THE
SCOURGE
OF
Liberalism
AND THE
UNIVERSAL LIE

THE
SCOURGE
OF
Liberalism
AND THE
UNIVERSAL LIE

JACK HALL

The Scourge of Liberalism And The Universal Lie

iUniverse books may be ordered through booksellers or by contacting:

iUniverse
1663 Liberty Drive
Bloomington, IN 47403
www.iuniverse.com
1-800-Authors (1-800-288-4677)

ISBN: 978-1-5320-0483-4 (sc)
ISBN: 978-1-5320-0484-1 (e)

Print information available on the last page.

iUniverse rev. date: 08/18/2016

CONTENTS

GENEALOG

*H*ere, where this once embattled nation fired the shot heard round the world, a multi-cultural existential Liberalism now destroys the traditional values it wrought. Likewise, where the moral redoubts once stood in defense of a Judeo-Christian inspired freedom, a wailing wall looms amid the mud and scum of political correctness. This is a harsh indictment for a nation of scientifically engineered realism that adroitly proclaims man not as a child of God but as the hierarchical remnant of simian progeny. Still open for debate is whether their creation specialists of Darwin and Freud, instead of scouring the south seas in search of our lineage, should have laid claim the archipelagos ahead of the Chinese malediction. This would have allowed more constructive time to train the simian fledglings on how to deal with the natural law of "conflict" before Marx divided the ill-educated masses into the zoomorphic halves and halve nots. Because heaven is not a "thing" but of a divine negative charged spirit essence, where no fact of objective matter can dissect its cause, was not reason to obfuscate its ineffable vestal modesty. Never to focus a child's attention to the diametric extremes of the all perfect and pure in unity with the archaic and ignoble defied symmetry of reason. To bar from knowledge the term "freewill" as man's only means for crossing the great divide to commune in the intimacy of truth through faith was an anathema of liberal bias. Today a teacher would be fired if they opened a childs dual hemispheric mind to revel in the negative pure mathematics responsible for the four pillars of Earth, air, fire, water, the atom building block and its electron generator of all earthly phenomena.

Facing the most important election of our time to curtail the decadence of an Eden II enlightenment the "have nots" ballyhoo the problem to the old Marxist adage "its economic inequality stupid." On the other extreme the outsider "haves" who want their country back from the liberal leviathan are pleading "let's make our simian nation great again with good trade deals and fences. Somewhere a stately baboon ruminates not about a fence but about his ill-educated progenitors who believe societies flourish because of man generated economics and discards the fact that "it's all providential stupid."

Today's rank judgment conjures the need to cast an eye to the forbidden fruit of the tree whose axis represents a heaven and hell unity. For whether of inanimate tree or simian spinal axis unless both are in alignment to creative oneness their being is useless.

Soon to grace the birthplace of freedom is the 400th anniversary of short memoried paradisal framing of the famed Mayflower compact. A never to be repeat epoch long since recycled of freedoms planting in America, the inspired seeds

2

for self-government and the advancement of the Christian faith in God, Amen. This colossal anniversary carries with it the same trepidation as when the nation awoke in 1957 to learn that orbiting the Earth was the first ever Russian born satellite Sputnik. It is not the recurrence of the Russian satellite that approaches to coincide with the Mayflower compact but the 1917 hundred year commemoration of freedoms greatest enemy of communism. That violent Russian revolution marked by overthrow, death, destruction and redistributive failed policy contained a manifesto sworn to defeat American Capitalism by the "united front" menace. As we peruse the landscape and grovel at the violent protests overtaking the nation, which of the following resound of jubilation? The freedom inspired Mayflower compact or the anarchist and thugs poised to elect a socialist and replace Capitalism with a Marxist style tyranny already underway.

What should concern us all is how the indoctrinated youth of utopian promises who brought to power the likes of Castro, Hitler, Mao and Stalin are once again ill-educated and deceived to become tomorrow's pawns of authoritarian tyranny.

Having lived through the Golden age of the most faith driven freedom inspired Christian enlightened world envy and to have seen this estranged benefactor of God undergo a spiritual lobectomy is like reliving Gethsemane.

The vanity of vanities rests with those who still believe that the guiding hand and loving face of freedom in spite of our evil ways still divine its protective shield.

As with all seeds physical, living and cultural they must atrophy, decay and die for rejuvenation of things eternal. Nothing occurs from nothingness and the spirit that gives birth can also cause the tenderest of heart its heaviest mourning when joy turns to shame.

This narrative rails against the two most sacrosanct idols that have short-circuit the culture. They are a political liberalism and its existential mentor of science. Both have conspired to lay waste the natural laws of freedom inspired, Christian enlightened, individual incentivized, limited government Eden II model. Both terms; political liberalism and existential science rear their ugly heads by observing the introductory symbol of the only absolute willed to man. They represent the positive or plus symbol that is bond to the central axis diametric the negative retractive universe that retreats ever purifying itself into the pure realm of divine perfection. A liberal existential atheistic science that believes matter precedes essence is contrary to the American founding principles. At the outset it is necessary to parse the syntactic meaning of science to affirm that the word science is a non-sequitur. There is no such thing as science. There are only sciences that factually cover every institution of a culture. Many will enlighten the world in the fields of medicine, materials, horticulture, biology, zoology, optometry, space, engineering, computer, robotics, atomic energy, soil, geology, weather, food-preparation, dental, applied and the list continues into anything factually revealing of nomenclature. None however have been able to prove one causal truth of its existence as freedoms way of preserving the ideal from the corruptible real. In our plight as corporate clones should we not by political correctness also declare as a quasi-science those fields such as tax evasion, bank robbing, illegal immigration, societal welfare, cyber hacking, drug running, gang violence, student visa fraud,

LBG trans-genderism, pornography addiction., occultism, humanitarian existentialism, sport enthusiast or terrorism.

All of the above semantical confusion was to single out the one unmentioned "black sheep" that has shamed an honest profession by using imperfect fact to falsely redefine the creation because of a bitter hatred for God and Christianity. Instead of locking arms with the cynosure all perfect to assuage the faithful, they will wage war on a total universe because it was impervious to factual proof. The following diagrams must prove beyond all doubt why we of the mutable and imperfect setting hinged to the eternal and resolute of intellect, having lost the shield of freedom, must begin to ask who was the prima-facie instigator of a terror that has come full circle.

Amidst the white-wash of scourge a rudderless nation reserves for death what the faithful must learn face to face as follows.

(A)

The creation according to God

Two opposing worlds – one positive charged of matter whose essence is gravity unified to the ion generative negative charged of pure essence. The central axis whose cusps are bond to the invincible electro-magnetic ellipse represents the only absolute number in creation able to bond to one side the positive symbol and directly opposite the negative extreme of minus one. Electro-magnetism which is responsible for all creative phenomena in form and motion is now bisect of truth and the absolute expunged in order to destroy belief in God.

(B)

The universe according to science

One autonomous evolved material sphere independent from natural laws of celestial origin. Because no objective fire annealed fact can prove the nature of God or any causal truth the negative electron wave and a total pure subjective knowledge has been confiscated and adulterated as of matter origin. From the preceding symbol of the annulled absolute the terms liberal and conservative stand out in graphic detail. The central axis which represents the only number in creation able to expose the fire annealed positive charged Earth whose language, math, and objective imperfection is destined to atrophy, decay and die for rejuvenation of pristine beauty. Directly opposite is the obliterated negative energy sphere whose infinite mathematics, intellect and trans mutational power that we of a charred imperfect sense can barely imagine. Once we realize that only because of the diametric extremes of positive and negative one the creation was able to become non dimensional, timeless, and of absolute pure quality in energy, intellect and law. Now interject that a spirit emanates from Earths fiery positive charged beginning and we arrive at a unilinear material bias whose learnings are liberal, existential, atheistic and paganistic. By definition all of the above believe that existence precedes negative essence, and that matter has precedence over mind and fact over faith.

Do not regard anything referenced on the absolute to infer that to be of the liberal persuasion is somehow bad. On the contrary this is a world of opposites and the great challenge is for unity not compromise of difference. All of us in our adolescent stage are material and liberal and unless the proper education introduces us to a dual world antagonism many lives are thrown to the wolves of fake motivation. Even in my own family of which I love dearly I am outnumbered and must tread lightly and replace discourse with conciliation. It is not unnatural to become enthralled with things and success in a land of opulence before those golden years of feeling eternal revert, as opposites will, to our regrets. To go through life without first capturing the faith to buttress the fact, never will anyone know the best of both worlds and a joyful end.

We should not wonder why the governor of one of our largest states has pronounced civil law having dominance over natural law. Because the coveted constitution was fortified with the divine precepts of natural law and the commandments of Moses made it vulnerable in the war against God.

Only one means gave the liberal existential enemies of God the power to destroy and claim victory over the absolute. That was by an ill-educated citizenry of corrupt body and soul under influence of the compelling lie. Many of the erudite of liberal and political persuasion will detest my defense of God and Christianity claiming that religious bigotry is the greatest cause of crime against humanity. Surely the great wars to defeat a worldwide tyranny had at its core enmity against the Jew, Christian and the cruel peace of Versailles. The communist threat since WWII continues to drain the blood and treasure because of a Godless ideology. And now the brutal terrorist slaughter that is bent on eliminating the Jew, and Christian as infidels of the Islamic faith is rooted in religious bias. THIS BOOK IS A WAKE UP CALL TO EITHER CAPITULATE AND COMPROMISE THE TRUTH OF FREEDOM OR DIE IN WORD AND DEED OF ONE WHO SENT US IN ITS DEFENSE.

This war will not be won by ideology, military strategy or social and economic condescension. Freedom cannot exist without the divine precepts of moral Christian law embodied in the world's greatest inspired constitution. Although the founders held grave reservation on a citizen will to preserve it, nothing ever existed before as an example for safeguarding life, liberty, property, happiness and the restraint of authoritarian tyranny. For this reason the erudite patriots who are pressing for a convention of states to reinvigorate the constraints of a mobocracy, the need is to first blot out the unconscious blight of sin that has dulled the senses and destroyed our national immunity. God pity us all in our pitiful state where the word sin is exempt from a fire annealed objective freedom.

Throughout history in times of moral crisis the antidote of divine shock and awe has appeared to purge the fool and save man form the Lords of Hell. Examples include the great deluge, the plaques of Egypt, Moses and the ten commandments, Shems tower of Babel scattering, Sodom and Gomorrah, Jesus of Nazareth, the advent of Christianity, the American Eden II freedom enlightenment, Bartholdi's Statue of Liberty, Borglum's Mount Rushmore, defeat of a world tyranny by freedoms greatest generation, the DNA revelation of Gods handprint in the human gene, Gods sifting of the Tea Party patriots and recent discovery of Gods "literal" plan of creation. Neither complete nor overshadowing are the thousands who recount of personal intercession in masterful invention and prophetic word.

Unfortunately all of the above because they lack factual objective proof have been sidelined as yesterday's myths. This will allow a liberal existential atheistic science and its professional brigand to bisect heaven from earth by instituting a new philosophy of freedom that excludes God.

FREEDOM

To have allowed the existential God hating liberal enemies of God to bastardize and transform this divine principle of natural law was treasonous. Before the creation came to be freedom already was as the most powerful word and force for restraining and allowing harmonious unity between a heaven and hell conflicting difference. For education to annul its true description as the suppressor and constrainer of evil for one of compromiser of moral principle was an anathema of the lie. For those erroneously led to believe that freedom is a principle of man's objective law ask yourself the following: By whose law was the rotation and revolution of all cosmic object aligned to perpetual form and interdependent motion? And by what mathematical freedom does day turn into night, summer to winter, the tides to rise and trough and the things of earth to atrophy, decay and die to eternal rejuvenation? Is it the natural law of freedom, as the essence of God that distributes an equal apportionment of light and darkness over the entire earth or is it man's civil law of the jungle concept of freedom? And which law of freedom was handed down to Moses that became our cornerstone of the constitution that respects the freedom to live, worship, own property, and pursue happiness? For certain it was not the bestowed freedom of government to willfully destroy life or make it a matter of choice, nor the freedom to transport the most vile of pornography over the sacred electron wave into every home and call it art. Neither was it their freedom to regulate the ones preference of belief regarding race, religion, ethnicity, political persuasion or to gerrymander communities for equality standards.

In the final amalgam it will be freedom "the pure" that will pass judgment on the poisonous civil weed that refused to teach a dual language, one of objective corrupt freedom and another eternal and morally perfect. To believe the evolution atheist that claims man is both freedom and God was to defame truth as the dishonest lie. For education to espouse the rot that right and wrong, good and evil spawn from a common root and not admit that evil evolved from hell was blasphemous. What a fool's paradise we've created which despises the Christian doctrine which says "Be charitable, love your neighbor and take the rugged path instead of conforming to the Marxist reliance on the comrades of government. All reliance today is on the probabilities of the imperfect fact of science and a caretaker enemy of freedom central leviathan. This most powerful icon of a mimetic science lies at the heart of why America never became the moral model of a destined universal freedom. Kudos to the liberal existential scientific atheist for an inventive genius that made us the manufactured pawns of a digitalized reliance on corporate things present and the transgressions of governing power.

In this secondary world of the real in things, something in the silent of unproductive is always doing us for reasons we know not what. When the thought is of good its opposite is there to give challenge and for the reverse the same is true. From the introductory symbol of the absolute it is evident that on the sentient battlefield of the mind two forces, one from below that is positive ground and another from above negative and pure is vying for sovereignty.

Freedom, the most powerful force of natural law was first breathed to restrain earths fiery beginning to validate a heaven and hell creation. Discount the foolish babble that earths genesis evolved from an explosion of gas and dust or from a cosmic collision. If you've never ventured into the mind's eye to retrogress into non-dimension, timeless and matter less pure conative energy and intellect of perfection, you are a slave to matters chaos. What happened to the adage "speak to the earth and it will teach you: who remembers that non-union instructor funded by the natural law of faith that construct the greatest Eden II paradise of the face of Earth. A freedom coded visionary of pure science who sanctified the vilified barons of oil, steel, coal, coke, the railroads and associate industries alongside the greatest generation to defeat the world's greatest tyranny unequaled in the annals of time. Take time to walk in the shoes of the God-send of those like my wife's father and his four brothers who went off to preserve the freedom that has since become denatured of its Godly quality. And if you, like the present First Lady, bemoan living in a house built by slaves meet my grandfather. A Cossack, who emigrated from Russia to spend his waking moments in the underground caverns, often on his back, mining the black gold that was needed to smelt the iron-ore for Carnegie's steel industry. His walk of over five mile to and from the mine each day illumined by a carbide lamp on his hat, activated by spit, served as his light source in the darkened caverns of a pick and shovel existence. On days he mined rock to get to the vein of coal he received no pay. When fortunate enough to mine coal he received 25 cents a car of probably a ton removed by mule. Always under the fear of cave-ins and Sulphur gas they relied on the canary in the morning and when the rats scurried they too sensed danger and followed to safety. In those laissez-faire days of "hands off for government" it was the soil and the soul that fortified the will of a good and penitent people to non-government Mason jar dependence. Only a Steinbeck or Michener could do justice to the beautiful farmette and wonderful family of six daughters and 2 sons. On weekends to watch him cut his spacious fields of hay by hand, then rake and bundle the grain to feed his cows and other animals would today be considered sub-human. And that was just a sideline before concentrating on turning the soil and planting the miracle seed into a spectacle of nature's bounty, where a mothers saintly hands, await preserving its God giving sustenance in the family larder. This brief synopsis of an inspired faith in natures law begs the question of how did we become a government dependent civil law of liberal existentialist who has turned good into evil? Who with animus for God and Christianity place all reliance on the civil law of man and freedom without a virtuous God? Whose stature in the world has devolved to where our allies no longer trust us and our most defiant enemies no longer fear us.

A nation whose liberal lion of the Senate mastermind repeal of the 1965 Immigration Act – reversing allocation of 85 percent to the most cultural unassimilable as to forever jeopardize the traditional standards of our heritage.

What nation offers untold numbers of NI Visas to students and foreigners who overstay the allotted time frame and are never surveilled as to why? And what nation releases from prison its convicted prisoners unconditional and many having committed serious felonies? Couple this to the program called "fast and furious" whereby high power weapons were issued to cartel and drug gangs again unsurveilanced and which were used to commit heinous crimes.

Chronolog

*C*reation was not intellectually intended as a cause for religious distraction. Neither is God a religious inference but a descriptive pronoun for which none greater exists to explain the creation. Evolution is neither a cause nor a law of anything except a subterfuge of reason that refuses to accept that a heaven and hell unity is responsible for the natural law of evolving conflict. The evolutionist refuses to associate good and evil with natural law that is why they refuse to recognize the negative charged universe as the primary generative ionizing absolute and have changed its nature to being of positive charge. The four pillars of positive earth and negative water are opposites as are positive fire and negative air. They are not religious combatants and with the proper education we should follow suite. By refusing to teach the dual language of the positive imperfect conceived in fire and the negative pure of eternal quality has become our nemesis. Of critical importance let us consider; were words created for the sake of things objective, or were things created for the sake of descriptive words? On this query rests the future of American freedom in its death struggle with its liberal avowed scientific affirmed unilinear evolved material creation by happenstance, absent a beginning. Generations have been led to believe falsely that man is the inventor and creator of the language and its mathematics. Should a child ask they are told that language began with the grunts and groans of animals or was first copied from the walls of ancient caves. This confirms what most are led to believe that things of object were created for the sake of words. For certain the unilinear material evolutionists who believe existence precedes essence would concur. As a nation of political correct liberal interpretation of freedom we allowed educators to direct all knowledge to a matter over mind, fact over faith rationale. That allowed for the most destructive liberal lie ever foist on the innocent mind that described freedom as wearing only one face. An objective fire annealed genesis that exempt all things from restraint. Never mentioned was the pure eternal first breathed to stem earth's fiery beginning and which aligned all cosmic form to perpetual motion. None of which was possible without first restraining all conflicting impediments of evil opposition. What a sham to leave a child with the impression that earth, air, fire, water and the miracle elements of atom all appeared out of evolutionary nothingness to await the great simian God to give them defining word. What creator would be so foolish?

A nation that fails to look first for the essence of the word that created the object is an ill-educated ignorant buffoon. Taken one step further would it be too shocking to reveal that before each of us came to be, the word was already within us from conception, to extol the illusions of false motivation. To evade teaching a child that the vital soul is a non-religious unifying function of a dual being only exacerbates the corruption of the corruptible body. In that same vein, to evade mention of God because of an objective religious bias was criminal. The word God is an intellectual concept of erudite reason beyond which no greater concept exists. And to perceive of an overarching ineffable, unexplainable perfection of a mathematical superstar, thank God for use of his word of name that explains all things.

The more advanced a civilization becomes the more critical is the need for cultural cohesion; not by oppressive rules but by incentivized opportunity. Governments have one purpose, national security and equal justice under natural law. As freedoms greatest enemy they produce nothing except unending reams of restrictive legislation in the quest for equality which doesn't exit. When the diversity of science and government become as one they become God and they become freedom. Natural law is replaced by the civil law of the jungle and the culture rots internal. Both government and science live by the personal opinion of imperfect fact then report it as probable truth.

Both will follow and believe in Darwin's theory of natural selection in which the species evolved overtime through adaptation. Darwin believed the traits of two parents were blended like the mixing of paint. Not so, by natural law. Genes are handed down by segregation of gametes with one factor from each parent. If a black cat is blended to a white cat the end result is a grey kitten. The truth is that the species was not independently created by natural selection. Another area of controversy is over the estimated time needed for the earth to cool. Lord Kelvin estimated it took

400 million years based on current temperatures. Other physicists were estimating that it took billions of years based on radioactivity. My conclusion is if we eliminate personal opinion based on imperfect fire annealed fact and project everything to non-dimension, non-objective, timelessness we must conclude that the word freedom automatically cooled and instantly readied the earth for the atoms birth in timeless pure mathematical precision.

Absolute positive and negative one is our only assurance on earth that anything exists by the natural law of opposites. That leaves us with the first law of human nature which is "to know thyself."

How masterful and defiant of words is this secondary creation designed from the diametric extremes of a heaven and hell contrast, then bequeathed to a neophyte junior likeness of both that defies comprehension. With nature as his guide and emulating model, required the unity of sense and essence or suffer to hells conflict. His five material senses unless bond to the generative ionizing soul, as with any seed, short circuit one's ability to harmoniously ripen, mature and die to the partition of both worlds.

For science, as the icon of earth, to destroy a creative plan and its ineffable planner, first had to destroy a beginning. This infraction, which will divorce generations from the truths of heavens subjective knowledge, will poison education and make us the outcasts of creation subject to the horrors of chaos.

The story of creation is best explained by the example that everything is a miniature seed replica of the creative plan. Although no eye has ever seen the atom it is an embryonic seed of positive charged matter circumscribed and ionized by infinite numbered negative charged electron. It has been postulate to be of such incalculable density that the words positive and negative can only emanate from a supernatural mind. J. D. Jukes in his book *Man Made Sun* calculates that one hundred million atoms, from which each is composed of two anti-atoms of positive and negative force, could be placed end to end around the outer edge of a postage stamp. And of its infinitude of negative pure number of 107 known seed programmed to pollinate individually and cross pollinate to form a ubiquitous variety is a miracle beyond comprehension. Our best description of the atom cell is from science whose probes in search of cosmic truth reveal that what they observe from the depths of space is no different from observing the human cell.

With this, let us return to the short circuit material bifurcators of a dual creation and observe how an ignorance of the natural law of conflict, arising from diametric extremes, has fueled the demise of Eden II America. Once the words God is transmute to living flesh as an admonition of truth, its seed of Christianity aligned to freedom will jettison the world's greatest moral movement. Every living seed by natural law and imperceptible to the human eye will inauspiciously sprout its deceptive weed to choke the good of existence. Should we not expect the materialist evolutionary weeds of an atheistic earth science to sprout in opposition to its spiritual competition.

On one path out of the middle age spiritual enlightenment will be the negative inspired visionaries on a mission of faith to a divine will. On another is an opposing brigand timed to a rising industrial age dedicated to a material utopia based on a redistributive equality for all. If there was one fly in the ointment of the latter it was their ignorance of not knowing that by natural law nothing in all of creation was equal nor ever would be except in death. Recent Russian experiments now show that no two snowflakes are identical which if true should close the case and accept the prophetic words that "the poor will always be with us."

Ask yourself was it by fact or by faith or because things exist because of the word that the faithful visionaries will after severe persecution and internal dissension set sail for a preordained mission. Or, that the latter opposition steeped in an alien Marxist God hating ideology will also head north then veer right and end up in Russia. One was on a journey to sow the seeds of an American inspired Eden II enlightenment of world envy, and another conflicting weed of evolution, revolution and the transformation of freedom into an authoritarian Marxist worldwide tyranny.

Few are alive today to remember the scopes trial when the law against teaching of Darwin's evolution was challenged. Although scopes was found guilty the "monkey trail" will arouse the liberal weed to surface in promoting academic freedom and advance the "survival" of the fittest theory with man a wonder of the new world monkey. When I entered school in the late 1930's almost every blackboard displayed the life size stages of man's evolution from the hunched over old world to the new world upright simian. This occurred prior to the Great Depression which dove-tails to the Great War to preserve freedom from a worldwide tyranny. The spoils of that war will bring the two aforementioned forces of a freedom inspired Christian enlightened good into its death struggle with those of a wartime communist ally dedicated to a Marxist anti-God destruction of the capitalist system.

Never before chronicled are the spoils of the Great War from which neither victor nor vanquished was immune.

First as a national wonder the mother will be jarred from the home to fill a workplace vacancy never to be returned. Her departure along with the advent of television and an ongoing war against God and Christianity, made her the ideal art form and be enjoined to the electron wave fascination for the erotica. And because it was her embryonic seed as the atoms model to receive the miracle of negative charged essence, the 1973 Supreme Court repeal of abortion laws in 46 states allowed for her sacred womb to be violated for what was considered as lifeless chattel. Keep in mind that the present rate of aborted fetus, (the improvised animal name for life) has now reached an annual rate surpassing one million.

Other disturbing spoils of that war will involve tensions with our wartime Russian ally. After signing the treaty of peace of World War II Germany will be divided into four quadrants each occupied by the allied powers. Russia will receive the fourth zone which included E. Berlin and the Eastern Bloc countries she had previously overrun. Animosity arose between Stalin and Roosevelt because of not sharing the secrets of the Atom bomb and refusing them a share of Japans occupation because of their failure to enter the war until American victory was eminent. This will lead to the soviet refusal to grant free elections in the agreed to Eastern Bloc countries leading to a cold war. After a thousand mile barrier from the Baltic to the Adriatic that will cut Europe in half. Churchill will proclaim it as a Russian iron curtain. While America is busy aiding war-torn Europe with the Marshal plan the communists will instigate unfinished wars of aggression to destabilize the world's superpower.

THE CONFLICT OF CHAOS

*I*n this magnificent creation where the mutable is governed by the eternal, the human seed like the flower, must ripen, decay then die lacking all surety of anything. According to Lord Tennyson, "if we knew the flower, roots and all, we would understand creation." My contention is that we must first understand the word which pre-empts the seed of the root. That procedure required not gravitating to earth in search of answers but searching outward for the words that made earth its vassal. Was not the DNA miracle, which is only five percent made productive, the pre-ordained word that explains our every aspect of development. Should this not be true for all things? No word in the language of man, because it is least understood, has turned the worlds most enlightened freedom inspired nation into a fool's paradise, on the way to demise. That word is the natural law of conflict which is the balance wheel, for a freedom inspired Christian enlightened envy of the world. Conflict which will accompany us with our first breath and aligned to death will be with us when we take our last. We cannot understand the natural law of conflict unless we have knowledge of duality, a term the evolutionists will remove from a child's education. In its place the "matter over mind" liberal existential will interject the atheistic views of three lemming misfits. Their surreptitious names form the bedrock of our modern guilded education whose opulence bankrupts the nation in abstract fool's gold. A brief summation of why the culture rots because of their reasons for conflict are (A) because of economic inequality, (B) an infantile sexual neuroticism and man's evolutionary struggle to define himself. Before this deranged culture takes its last gasp in dire surprise, pause to the truth of conflict.

DUALITY

$\mathcal{A}$ simple word which means two is not my invention but transcends to the more brilliant intellect of ancient Greece. Some things are self-revealing and anyone, who possesses the stereoscopic miracle of sight, can reason that an over-arching celestial absolute has dominance over the mutable and corruptible of earth. To contrast both and not sense that this unified perfection is governed by natural law and not man's civil law is short circuit in reason. Natural law is eternal and rigidly set to a negative pure mathematics that governs all form and perpetual motion. By natural law nothing is equal, no two snowflakes, no two DNAs, no two anythings except in death are we equal. Never taught is the pure language of natural law of which the word beauty is the personification of difference. Natural law is about infinite mathematics, pure energy and conative power of which because of a dual heaven and earth unity we struggle to comprehend. Try to envision the natural law of non-dimension, timelessness and non-existence. Whatever you decide, after the realization that nothing happens on its own, add the two words never explained that is proof positive of a dual creation. Those words transmute from the immutable pure and made real in an unexplainable creative miracle are positive and negative force. From the introductory symbol positive explains the real of matter whose essence is gravity, and negative essence as the ionizing generator of all form and function. When unified in oneness we know the resulting phenomena as electro-magnetic force. The election wave as the nursemaid of God, that transcends the depths of matters hell has destroyed every factual probe of science in its search for cosmic truth.

To ask what does the above have to do with the conflict of chaos that has been falsely defined and superimposed onto our culture that now rots internal.

- A. Conflict is a universal result of the natural law of the creative heaven and hell diametric extremes of difference. This has nothing to do with man, his evolutionary struggle or some psychological sexual neurosis.
- B. Conflict arising from opposites was Gods way of using competitive rivalry to learn from a capricious foe the difference between good and evil. And according to the stevedore philosopher Eric Hoffer, conflict with a capricious nature was necessary to occupy man from dying out.
- C. The conflict arising from a heaven and hell rivalry proves that by natural law freedom in the true sense in a restrainer of the conflict of chaos, if not by freedom what force can dissipate the fires of hell into perfected substance. It was a lesson for the

evolutionists that freedom was not intended to make compromise with the conflict of evil. Anyone who follows the downward pull of gravity in search of a material utopia, by following Marx, Darwin and the fraud, place their trust in a central cyclops to do their bidding for collective equality, multicultural utopianism, and a fact over faith atheism. None of what they prophesy speaks to the origin of anything except the inane theory that it occurred by happenstance out of nothingness. Seldom do they except the deists claim of a prime mover, and if they do sense that a mind spirit created the universe, that it did so for man to manage.

For certain the natural law of a dual creation destroys man as God and man as freedom by the simple analogy of the weed and the seed. A dual language, one of object and another of primary descriptive subject is omnipresent in the seed that gave us conception. Before the creation, there was only the unsoiled infinite number that contained within itself, in the same manner as our own DNA, the true essence of a freedom inspired form. We know that every atom seed of which no human eye has ever seen is composed of a positive matter embryo or gamete, united to a circumscribing electron ionizing generative spermato of spirit essence. Every atom is composed of a positive and negative anti-atom stabilized by a neutron balancing stem except in the first offspring we know as hydrogen, which is on a one to one basis. This inequality of the building block atom is proof that the conflict of opposites pervades all existence.

My purpose in this narrative is to begin with the example of the good seed that is always shadowed by the destructive weed that mysteriously appears to choke what the soul has sown. Let us begin with the atom seed of dual conflict and trace it to the human seed where it outcrops in the opposites of man and woman, love and hate, freedom and tyranny, hot and cold, good and evil, life and death, war and peace, fact and faith, matter and essence, ignorance and wisdom, health and sickness and finally a liberal existential matter over mind vs. the complete, all perfect, negative pure absolute. In this dual creation where one world was made strictly for passing through, absent an effective instruction guide except natural law, left little time to get things right. Even our living associates of animal and plant would be muted to avoid confusion. That still put us in a catch 22 between the resources of earth that provided food and pleasure and from above the miracle of light, breath of air and transport of water as the staff of life. We could follow gravity and the material logic of man or put all trust of faith in God and balance the two. Not until the Hebrew prophesies came to fruition in the advent of Christ, will the miracle seed of faith, harvest a spiritual revolution. Christianity will provide the new humanity, beyond the grave, to challenge and bring to its knees the secular absolution of Rome. After the fall of Rome, it will be Christianity that will lead the downtrodden back to the living soil, to save man from extinction. After a thousand year humbling of revitalized soul to the nourishing seed of plenty, historians will pen this period of saving grace as the "Dark Ages". History books will be altered and the rise of Christianity blamed for a thousand year repression of objective learning. No text will infer that this was the staging area for a faithful avenger to transport freedoms co-equal Christian fortifying soul to an Eden II American enlightenment. In another staging area, an opposing seed is being harvested to choke the followers of a combined Jew and Christian monotheistic condemned conspiracy of eternal bliss with an invisible God.

A worldwide duality of opposites, one fueled by the spirit of hells material utopia brand as the Renaissance of science, and another the Dark Age avengers of hell's kitchen atonement of sin and its redemptive savior. The Christian faithful will head north out of Italy on a mission known only to the God of freedom. On another route north are the liberal existential socialist aggressors bent on a Marxist material utopia. To their advantage is the mercantile age of trade, discovery, settlement and the rising city states, facing the inequalities of an approaching industrial bonanza. You be the judge as to whether by choice or by freedoms prodding the corrupting weed of atheistic materialism will veer right out of Germany and end up in Russia. Even more eclectic is the enigma of the faithful vanguard who after suffering internal strife and external political persecution set sail on that dangerous journey to a virgin plantation. Which was most axiomatic of a guiding hand allegory come full circle today in the battle between good and evil.

THE DEMISE OF FREEDOM

*L*et us begin with the spoils of the communist masterminds of revolution, that we saw leave Renaissance Italy in the 15th century, on a mission to oppose the rising tide of Christianity. Instead of a faith in God theirs was a matter over mind, nationalized material utopia based on man as God and man as freedom.

While the Christian faithful were planting the seeds for a freedom inspired Christian enlightened Eden II America, the Marxist weed was not so lucky. After struggling to form a base among the disgruntled of labor and meeting opposition in Germany they will veer east and end up in Russia. We can only imagine what role freedom played in this wide displacement of bitter enemies. Here they will stage their 1917 revolution that will kill the Czars and begin nationalization of the land. Wide spread peasant revolts will occur with the burning of crops and destruction of livestock leading to mass deportations to Siberian Gulags. For our concern capitalism will be blamed for war, imperialism, militarism and social inequality among the masses. Their claim was that when hand implements under feudalism were turned into machines of the industrial age, the land owner of old became the wealthy barons responsible for the above atrocities. This liberal socialist sepsis is still freedoms constant tormentor. In the midst of their 1917 revolution they will declare death to capitalism by means of the "United Front" in their manifesto for its destruction. Fast forward to the Great War of which Russia will become our ally against the Nazi war machine, World War II was freedoms greatest triumph to defeat a world-wide tyranny of Americas might and greatest generation were nothing short of a stratagem of divine will. I was well positioned of age to testify of this freedom bred resourcefulness, in human and productive stature, unequalled in the annals of warfare. Unfortunately, I was also part of that golden age that saw the spoils of war as the avengers of freedoms cause returned home to recoil from the wounds of war and seize the pleasures of peace. Fortune however was not so kind knowing that the godless enemy was unsheathing the sword for unfinished wars of communist aggression.

In this world of conflicting opposites, that golden age of courageous American avengers of freedoms cause, returned home to their own Iliad and odyssey. As our ally during the war, the Russian bear was irate over our not sharing of the atomic secrets, and refusing her a role in the occupation of Japan. Europe would however be divided between east and west but her failure to enter the pacific conflict until the end was a wise decision on our part. Keep in mind that socialism and liberal existentialism are enemies of freedom and capitalism. Sworn to allow free elections in her Eastern European countries after the war were denied causing

Churchill to declare that an iron curtain was imposed from the Baltic to the Adriatic leading to the cold war. The word "cold" war was a deceptive term for what would become unending wars of communist aggression that would tear the fabric of freedoms defenders unlike ever before. 1950 will become the turning point of American valor in the brutal return to save South Korea from its invasion by the communist north. Never realizing that the Chinese would enter on the side of the north, left us with no choice but a humiliating truce that sixty plus years later we are still there. From Korea in will be Vietnam under the same scenario that will tear the country apart with protests over the war and riots for civil and human rights. During this same period Russia will place missiles in Cuba ninety miles from our shore leading to a nuclear showdown. The missiles will be removed but in the fog of stare down we will lose a president to assassination never able to fully connect the dots.

1953 will see the atomic secrets stolen by the Rosenberg spies and passed to the soviets. This wife and husband team will be executed although this will give the enemy the advantage of discovery of the H Bomb ahead of us. 1954 saw rumors abound that the communists had infiltrated the highest reaches of the State Dept. during the war. Add to this that the "avowed to destroy capitalism" United Front under the aegis of freedom was now entrenched in the labor movement, higher education and the political movement with a nominee for president. Finally enough concern mounted to hold Senate sub-committee hearings on the threat. These would become the first ever televised hearings of which, as a driver of the company commander in those days, was able to watch the proceedings to my dismay and many others. Similar to today's hearings on top secret e-mail groundless accusation, the McCarthy hearings made him out to be a villain and a fool ruined of image, and confined to an early death.

By giving the communist adversaries a free pass the first amendment protection of natural law of speech, press and religion was not so fortunate. A Supreme Court volley will be fired into the heart of freedom as the essence of God and Christianity as its moral standard bearer. I was there when school prayer and bible reading would exit education and eventually the public forum. To not reason that starting a child's day with the purifying blessing of our faith and not relate it to the first glimmer of light or sun that precedes the day is a fool. Who among us remember the vacuum that was left when God departed, ushering in a bizarre culture of drugs, sex, rock and roll, all of which has destroyed the system as wasting mind fields of abstract nothingness?

And should you ask how did this happen to freedoms greatest? And only one answer suffices. It is called liberal, existential, atheistic evolutionary icon of the scientific method. Should you care to know when, reflect to 1957, a day that the enemies of freedom produced the weed that would choke the seed of Eden II America. That morning along with the light of day the nation awoke to the trepidation that a soviet satellite, the first ever, was circumnavigating overhead every sixty odd minutes. Any thoughts of Shem's tower into the realm of forbidden transit and its scattering soon evaporate to the human fear of unprotected vulnerability. Before the day was over it was the renowned newscaster Walter Winchell who railed that the American boy who could have pioneered such a feat was probably walking the street deficient in math and science.

Almost overnight science will become the unofficial headmaster of education. This will be the fuse that led to the 1963 Supreme Court ban on prayer and bible reading and the rise of an objective counter culture of freedom without God. Not since the Great War will American forces leave the battle field with head held high in victory, except for a short stint to save Kuwait from being overrun by Saddam Hussein.

Finally, after one hundred year of subtle and open conflict between the communist leaches of freedom and the inspired Christian and Jew capitalist the verdict is in and unless a miracle is pending it's not pleasant. Somewhere between the instigated wars of aggression and the race for the frontier of heavens area of forbidden transit the materialist invoked an ominous exclamation of pride. Instead of Christian spires that dot the landscape like pointed fingers of praise to God, the new vogue was of pointed hell fired spires awaiting command to obliterate whole nations. Rogue states now joined in the animus for Jew, Christian and hated capitalist. With God in abstentia and science busy conducting the affairs of climate and scouring the universe for other life overlooked another weed of freedom. This one hatched by hell in human flesh. This scourge with fake passports, social security numbers and bank accounts escaped radar to enter flight school not to fly but to steer passenger jets. Before that dreadful day would end; the world trade towers were demolished, the Pentagon attacked and over three thousand dead. Another plane loaded with passengers enroute for the capital was diverted by courageous passengers and forced to crash in S.W. Pennsylvania. Pause and reflect on the whence of freedoms protective shield.

THE TRANSFORMATION

In America, blessed with the grandeur of freedom as the essence of God, elections unveil ones conviction to preserve that honor. Not since our founding has the socialist indoctrinated leach of freedom made such inroads to spread its vile invective. 2008 was an extreme challenge, not only of ideology but to protect freedom from an accompanying economic tsunami that threatened a capitalist disaster. For the aspiring young Adonis with the oratory skills of a Daniel Webster, this was the challenge few presidents must face. His only vetting was as a community organizer and promise of hope and change which was vague in confident traditional expectations.

My critique is not meant to be personal, but to reflect on the motivations of an education and its indoctrinated associates of an alien liberal ideology. After all, the economic rebuke we faced was less a problem of greater government involvement when its roots involved freedoms long war between man and God, matter over mind, fact vs. faith, evil vs. good and freedom vs. tyranny. The day of freedom being impregnable to poisonous rhetoric was over. Unfortunately the leach of freedom had found a vulnerable umbrella to vent a civil law sepsis. Having taken the oath to uphold, protect and defend the constitution, during economic gloom, had some with cross fingered speculation. Doubt also began to abound over ideology, writings, birth and known radical associates. There were no canaries sent aloft to sample the "word matter" airwaves nor the long tailed rattus still tenured in the indoctrination cubicles disguised by exterior leaves of climbing ivy. Many were in wait to fill the pecking order to breathe a transformative justice to the conveyer belt of glooming regulation.

The first salvo for what lay ahead for hope came from the First Lady who bemoaned the need for cultural change and institutional reform. Shortly thereafter came her husband's claim that the constitution was too restrictive in its negative denials that restrict executive action. For the ill-educated and low information crowd this complaint mattered not, but for anyone of reason, this was a broadside against the freedom inspired Christian enlightened moral laws of Moses bound into civil law. Never doubt that it was the bill of moral rights tied to the Adam Smith Laissez-Faire individual incentivized absence of government control that built the greatest Eden II experiment on the face of earth.

That one insidious remark by the president, that the constitution was too restrictive in granting government power over the people, was a violation of the oath of office. Further proof of executive disloyalty came on a follow up "apology tour" to Egypt that insinuates America as a cause for world disorder. What effect this had on the Arab spring uprising that spawn a Pandora's Box across the Middle East is anybody's guess. The turning point of American hegemony would come with the withdraw of all American troops from a stable yet fledgling Iraq, without leaving a contingency status of force agreement. This would create a vacuum for the rise of radical Islamic terrorism as our greatest threat today. We would side with the Egyptian Brotherhood in their short lived overthrow of our long-term friend President Mubarak of Egypt. Next, their taking down of Gaddafi in Libya, and refusal to aid our diplomats who took residence in the annex of our embassy which came under terror attack, causing the loss of four brave Americans bordered on criminality. Then came the red line with Syria over use of chemical weapons which proved to be all smoke and mirrors that turned our allies against us and our enemies no longer to fear us.

As the Middle East turned into a tinder box, at home the failing economy was approached contrary to the Adam smith theory of "let nature take its course". Economic down turns are a principle of the natural law of supply and demand, production and consumption and the curative remedy is to bleed the system of its impurities, not to flush it with the antigen that destroyed the antibodies. It is after all competition that is freedoms cure for conflict and not the pump priming of inflationary fiat that pollutes the veins. We were facing the grim fact of watching the most freedom inspired system on earth devolve into socialist transformation. Many of the ill-educated believed that socialism was a more equitable form of democracy that shares the booty of the wealthy. Had they been educated to the belief that by natural law freedom endowed the individual through his labor of hand and resource of land as the worlds greatest egalitarian liberator of human misery.

Absent the long arm of government which is the enemy of freedom, America transcend to world envy because of this Adam Smith Laissez-Faire system of which means "let nature take its course". And that unbelievable course was to use competition as the secret to solving the natural law of conflict not as Marx advocated by allowing a central cyclops to redistribute the wealth. Under Laissez-Faire those who can't compete to produce the lowest price and better quality under the invisible hand of competition must find a substitute or leave the market place. This system produced an American Golden Age absent government subsidies, bailouts, massive regulation, or quantative easing that mired the country in generational debt for our children and massive borrowing that made our enemy the fiduciary of our assets. Look to China and reflect on the cover of Life or Time, back in the 50's, which in bold face proclaimed by Arnold Toynbee the famed British historian; "Beware the sleeping giant – and when she awakens, the world will tremble". Ask yourself what was the stimulus that awakened the giant and provided the secrets and finances that makes the capitalist tremble today.

In the past, the founder's solution for the scoundrels who hemorrhaged the system was to suffer the consequences. Then after a day of prayer and fasting and imploring freedom to purge the system marvels would occur. For example, the fan dancer scoundrel Fanny May and Freddie Mac would have exit the stage and with the politicians that created the blunder. Ask yourself what sane country would issue collateral free mortgages knowing they would turn into worthless derivatives that other scoundrels bundled for profit. Unfortunately the 2008 autocracy saw it differently and instead of reason they will pump prime the system with countless billions of taxpayer borrowed dollars. Millions will go directly to a failed industry that should have declared bankruptcy and left nature decide its course. Who remembers cars for clunkers and shovel ready jobs that forgot the shovels and green energy projects that only lined the swindlers pockets with green algae? As the debt escalates from six trillion to the near 20 trillion today, and manufacturing still anemic, prognosis is that ninety four million have left the work force and forty five million are on food stamps. With entitlements going broke and discretionary spending with no tomorrow what would happen should we be provoked into another war.

Somewhere in the mouse eared pages of "Rules for Radicals" the solution for the peaceful revolution must prescribe bailouts, quantitative easing, mounting debt and welfare give a ways as an adjunct to woo the drones to vote liberal for the transformation into a Marxist hell.

None of the above was possible unless the scientific method destroyed the truth of natural law and divorced heaven from earth and convert freedom into its material prototype without God. Once man extolled himself as freedom and as God, Christianity and its faith of soul became a clone of matters things. Take notice how the masses perambulate with devotion to the hand held small screen ever attracted to the world of science. No longer is there distinction between good and evil, true and false, honesty and dishonesty. No better example exists without a reflection to Lenin's transformation in Russia. His mistake was to begin by nationalization of the land and the industry. In America the liberal consortium, without one Republican vote, will nationalize the health care industry comprising one sixth of the G.N.P. Unlike resounding protests as occurred in Russia this takeover of peasant need was made possible by the stealth of bribes, kickbacks, secrecy and the cover of Christmas to pass a 2500 page manifesto which no one read. From behind the speakers dais the lady praetorian will giddily defend the thievery by announcing with a Bolshevik air; "We had to pass it so you could find out what's in it". For the opposition party who vehemently opposed the theft, they would be called domestic terrorists. Yet, in order to pass the manifesto it had to be buttressed to the lie that; you can keep your doctor, premiums and co-pays lower, it would be affordable, young people will find it attractive, it won't add to the debt, none of which was true.

Too vast to be called erring judgment, there was evil in the strategy that caused some to lament, "I hope he fails". Anytime the word strategy appears I am behooved to mention a notable associate that reverts to antiquity. After Sparta's failed ten year siege to conquer Troy to avenge the abduction of his wife Helen by Paris, son of the Trojan monarch, a cunning idea emerged. Who has not heard of the Trojan horse, filled with Spartan warriors and placed on the shore of Troy as a token of capitulation. Dragged inland under the cover of dark the soldiers disembarked and a great triumph of victory.

A lot has changed since Homers epic poem and if 2008 has any resemblance it is that instead of a hollowed out horse full of invaders the abbreviated stratagem laid out by Marx, Nietzsche, Alinsky and others was to hollow out the pre-frontal cortex and genetically engineer the lobes of conscious with the socialist propaganda of an Orwellian material utopia. Next turn the attention of the short circuit plebes to the new freedom that liberated a bottled up sexuality as the basis for civil law, quite a contrast with the divine precepts of freedom which required moral unity. Don't underestimate that revolutions can be peaceful and today's revolutionaries have been re-wired to the fiber optics of the digitalized chip called "Rules for Radicals". These social engineers have become entrenched in the rattus ivy studded incubators of the freedom without God scientific laboratories.

Nothing should disturb the conscience more than the thought that heaven has been unofficially bisect, God annulled and the heaven off limits except for flight and experiments in search of other life and defensive observation. We refuse to accept the natural law that objective fact conceived in matters hell, was forever denied crossing the line of demarcation, that separates object from subject to uncover one truth of creative phenomena. These same factual scavengers were immune from regulating the rhythmic cycles that kept the face of mother earth pure and eternal. For an absentee landlord it must have caused consternation to watch an enfeebled Lilliputian profess to be claimant over precisioned climatic cycles. After all, no fact could effectuate the complex invincible natural sensors that diffuse harmful solar x-ray and gamma radiation from entering earth, as well as harmful emissions ascending upward. Equally troubling to our guardianship must be the liberal existential brazen shut down of the coal industry. Carbon footprint is a contrived idiom since our bodies are composed of positive charged carbon in unity with three negatives of 75% hydrogen, oxygen and nitrogen. Carbon bodies emit CO_2 which is converted by plants into the oxygen we breathe which is a miracle of planning.

For the innocuous liberal existentialist to shut down the coal mines purposefully located in underground veins to supplement a substitute energy source and assist in the production of steel was no evolutionary "dead fossil" act of happenstance. These many varied mineralized deposits were laid down after freedom quelled the inferno and the apportionment of dual atom seed propagate to furbish the miraculous variety of earth. Etched on my memory during Americas Golden Age was being awakened each morning by the steam engine, pulling its twenty or more empty cars heading for the coal strippings.

They were also a sight to see after school as they left the town fully loaded on their way to the switch-backs down the mountain. What great effect they had on our ability to out produce the Nazi war machine cannot be denied. Unfortunately, it was not the carbon resource as the problem but the open pits that became a refuge for the city's sludge. The purpose of government was primarily to protect its people from poisoned underground aquafers and the lives it affected. Instead of micro-managing the lives of the citizenry how about closer scrutinizing where a city's sludge is being dumped and the artificial mountains of trash that harken to tomorrow's phantom plaque.

Has anyone considered that when a government refuses to identify and call the enemy its name as our greatest threat, that it has lost the will to govern. And it is not true that the reason why Americans have lost faith in their government is because government has destroyed the faith of its people. Has not the time arrived to call a halt to a socialist transformation and implore Godly freedom to repel the makeover and return his loving soul to refurbish an evil land?

In America once the oath is taken to preserve, protect and defend the constitution the word transformation is an anachronism that borders on dishonesty. For the office holder the process is one of style on how to administer the law according to the written blueprint. The only transformation is of party or faces and the reorganizing of office staff. To use the term I have a pen and a phone to execute a way around the law is a bold impulse of forethought. The liberal existential who views freedom as man ordained and not God inspired is an enemy of the constitution. A scientific annulment of a dual language, one of object and another of subjective quality, has become this nation's greatest impediment. Pure freedom, first breathed to stem the fires of hell and set all atomic structure to perpetual freedom, then align with the Judeo-Christian ethic for an Eden II enlightenment defies objective word. Today, we've destroyed the natural law of freedom which preempts the creation for the inane hell's kitchen improvisation. This election will determine the fate of the once great republic. When Benjamin Franklin upon leaving the constitutional convention was asked, "What have you brought? replied: "A republic if you can keep it". At our own presidential convention now underway that answer is eminently clear. We have failed to preserve, protect and defend it. When God and Christianity have been removed from the equation and conflict is not unified by moral competitive unity, then the weed of terrorism crosses the threshold to dwell unto death.

If we are to redeem our ignorance it won't be by economics but a return to honor the abandoned vicissitudes of pure and authentic creative freedom. Never taught and yet profoundly evident is that pure freedom as our protective shield, for a century and a half that held evil at bay is now crucified of word by the annulment of the Christian ethic. When the loving face and guiding hand of freedom exit the land the vacuum was filled by the liberal existential atheistic mind over matter scientific method politician, who has turned the nation inside out. Anyone who can look out on the resolute of eternal harmony and perfection and discount the mighty role of the freedom miracle is an enemy of the archetype. The best advice I can give to anyone of faith in a day when 24 – 7 the huxters pervade our lives with the snake potients is to instead implore freedom which stemmed the fires of hell, to stem the fires of our own ill-being. Beware, that God does work in mysterious ways. Once realizing that freedom is the essence of God, and the electron is the essence of every atom, and our bodies are composed of seventy five percent three negatives gases and one positive of carbon insures that we are two thirds spirit essence and one third corruptible matter. Did Methuselah who lived to be 187 years understand this or Enoch who lived over three hundred. If freedom delivered our ancestors out of authoritarian tyranny to the shores of America, it still exists to deliver us from the clutches of an atheistic hell. This nation is judged by its educated knowledge and until the absolute is its fountain stone of a dual language, one of imperfect object and another subjective and eternal of soullear enlightenment, it's over.

If one should direct the attention from a matter monism to a mind over matter conviction it is this: Everything of an atom seed creation confirmed by science as being of proton embryo circumscribed and ionized by the election negative essence reveals its own truth. That is that everything composed of the positive charged proton is confined to atrophy and decay into transformative quantity, while everything of the same seed of electron essence is destined for eternal quality. For those who believe that life terminates at death it probably does for them because of a metamorphosed electron soul. To not believe that our mission is to unite in the eternal with our genetic soul line is preposterous. If we transplant this logic onto the cultural seed that has bisect heaven from earth, annulled God and His Christian moral tenants, then teaches of a "Big Bang" material God, has ripened this nation for banishment. The wise must not follow the demonic insane into a material nothingness. To remove the words God and soul from a child's education because no fact of matters hellish beginning can explain them was ludicrous. To educate from a purely material syllabus was akin to throwing a child into an opulent pen with the hogs, to slosh in abject meaningless mire that had no hold on the mind. Today a liberal existential Godless villainy separates the citizenry from a freedom inspired American colossus to one of irreconcilable gloom. I lived through this world's Great Depression and never really felt its effects. There was great apprehension when the bank closed without notice and savings lost, never to reopen until a quarter century later. Similar to the aftermath when Rome fell, the spirit of freedom turned fear into the sweat of the annealing soil and in my town that became the unifying signature breast plate of every home. I remember Mr. Swabick coming by with his horse to plow and who could forget the saintly Mrs. Parks, the midwife who served as today's hospital for five dollars a delivery. Just imagine if Marx, Engles, Lenin, Alinsky and the rest of the socialist bandolier instead of blaming conflict on the risk taking halves and saw conflict as a natural law of freedom, the election of 2008 could have been a blessing in disguise. Just imagine that troops would have remained in a stable Iraq, Isil would be a non-sequitur, Egypt and Libya would be thriving resorts, Israel would no longer fear a nuclear Iran and the millions of displaced refugee living in peace. We cannot look out on the perfection of a physical miracle and not reason that on one of the many ledges of hell there exists the real carbon footprint on display.

One of the most perplexing questions I was asked while writing this was; we can never survive this terrorist onslaught because they're already here right? How do you answer someone who has never heard the dual meaning of freedom? My response is if freedom can turn night into day and winter to summer how much easier to stem the barbarian tide of ignorance. We must recognize the problem as the crucifixion of His holy word in the true meaning of absolute one, freedom, beauty, natural law, virtue, sense, essence, life, love, unity, conflict, soul, atom, electron wave, etc. To recognize that freedom, the most powerful force in the universe, was first breathed to stem hells fiery advent as a guarantee the absolute word of one would never be transformed by the liberal lie. Pure freedom cannot exist without Christianity as its moral force. Otherwise it would have been futile to send Christ on its behalf. America, without the foundational bedrock of freedom and Judeo-Christianity can never be transformed into anything except a centralized tyranny and worst enemy. That requires a multi-cultural, political correct sepsis be furloughed to the scrap heap for a revitalized assimilated conversion to our founding principles. Faith once again must be unified to fact, prayer and bible reading returned to education, abortion ended, and repeal of the liberal inane 1965 immigration act that destroyed a cultural unity for a political ploy. In education a teacher's freedom to again have the right to join in any fashion the local, state or national organizations without the unified standard of today. The NEA does nothing to foster quality except to build a financial war chest to elect liberal members of Congress. We must become selective in our immigration policy and those of law abiding Christian faithful who are here to counter balance the scourge of abortion. I believe an oath of allegiance should be their passport to citizenship. How soon until the embryonic body and its objective words lose all meaning in defense of pure freedom and time arrives to study faces instead. We had already reached the stage of madness when our elected leader or leaders retreat before their sacred pledge. Naturally, the liberal existential of an objective man made freedom is immune from overarching spirit dominance. Unless pure freedom essence absolves the mind from a matter only dependency there is no true happiness. When an administration seeks to transform the most equitable and moral envy of the world they are the emissaries of freedoms rival in hell.

Once science destroyed the theory of opposites and abandoned the natural law of incentivized individual freedom a centralized authoritarian cyclops saw industry flee the country, our secrets compromised, economic and social turmoil return and terrorism cross the threshold. Most disturbing was how the inventive mind of freedom continued to progress by designing a worldwide web, aligned to the electron wave, which the terrorist managed to encrypt, invade and mastermind a war of annihilation. The infant, who looks upon the mother as God, is more knowledgeable of truth, than all of an evolution guided science. This most adorable and beautiful of all flowering seed is reason alone that God is not only to be believed but understood. Our extolling of the butchers of science over the living infant is reason enough to explain why hell was a key ingredient of the creation. Just imagine if education spent its underlying syllabus on the knowledge of the seed. Inside every seed is a numbered genesis that is revealed of the greatest supernatural sculptor the world has ever known. Had science truly recognized the DNA as the most elegant and entrancing handprint of God, and not something put there by aliens. America would still be the shining city on a hill.

Few among us here ever reasoned whether the word was made for the sake of things and because we gravitate to the dishonest lie that things exist for the word of man, has transformed the meaning of truth. Each of us conceived of the positive and negative word of a transpiring belief begs the question of why some succeed in excellence and others feel estranged in a land of plenty. My belief is of a failure to unify the conflict of opposite by gravitating to the false god of matter and ignoring the essence of freedom with the adoration of thanks and praise has ruined many lives. We are surrounded by innumerable miracle of sun, stars, moon, light, life, color, birds, flowers, animals, food, family, etc. yet with every breadth how often do we unconsciously utter the words; praise God. Try it and once it becomes involuntary your life will be transformed and with it the beauty of what made the freedom inspired Christian enlightened Eden II the greatest nation on earth. Once we transform ourselves the liberal existential politician will hit a road block in transformation of the nation.

THE TRANSFORMERS LIE

*B*efore there could be a liberal transformation there had to be a wrecking crew who of mind were motivated to the real of matter over the ideal of essence. Such a crew were not adherents of the constitution but could easily be recruited from the Marxist manual, Saul's handbook or Sharia's website. Certainly, none would fit the popular housewives demolishers flip or flop that now grace most waiting rooms. These constitutional deconstructors attacked the infrastructure not from the basement where sewage or termite obstruction occurred but from the exterior buttresses that fueled the veins of its people. Instead of crow bars and hammers this refurbishing need only the pen and the phone and polluted word of an evolutionary hatred for the Judeo-Christian ethic of government. The 1963 Supreme Court decision to abolish school prayer left the genie out of the vial allowing for a half century time span to turn a population into sponge bobs for the new transfusion. The 2008 election salvo began by blaming the predecessor for all problems setting the nation up for a rebuke of war, imperialism, Abu Grab, Camp Gitmo, racial divide, carbon footprints, climate change and economic inequality and fortunately for the new transformers the scientific method had sanitized education in advance of a Judeo-Christian protest. These praying mantises came to lure the sluggards and drones through giveaways that gave notice that their savior had arrived to redistribute the wealth. Isn't that why the Roanoke colony under Sir Francis Drake vanished because of a government funded enterprise? And has not that same concept caused 95 million to vanish from the American work force and over forty five million to cop out on food stamps. Under freedoms law of incentivized individualism, absent government we've become the new colony of the strange word "Croatan" meaning Eden II banishment. We had evolved into a socialized demon instigated penal colony on the way to demise. So if this election has any meaning it is to nullify every liberal and their redistributive policy of a poverty provoked sepsis. The best advice I ever received from a freedom inspired saintly mother was to never envy people of wealth. That lesson became engrained having worked for millionaires who made it in coal, brick and hosiery. Five were brothers who had offices in the empire state building and in Switzerland during the Golden Age. What I saw was marriages ruined, children's lives left unstable and all left the world in dismay except one whose faith made him a pillar of the town. Another wealthy coal operator whom I admired came home one day to find his son had shot his own wife in the back yard. Another who came into town each morning with a beautiful blond at his side and like the others, stopped in for the morning paper and sundry items where I worked. After exhausting the six foot veins of coal and heading back to his home state, would on a foggy morning, kill several students at a bus stop. The one I ended up working for after high school as one of the finest multi-millionaires I ever knew, and who I would learn years later had passed leaving only misery for the wonderful children I once knew. So beware of a hidden duality in not only wishing for but entrusting an authoritarian demon of the dust as your administrator of a false equality of which only time is the equalizer.

The 2008 transformers and its point man lay his groundwork for change by the extractions of his "apology tour" to explain to the world that America was the instigator of world turmoil. What this did to inflame the Arab spring that erupt throughout the Middle East is anyone's guess. We will side with the Egyptian Brotherhood in their short lived overthrow of president Mubarak of Egypt, a longtime ally. Next came the withdrawal of all troops from Iraq leaving a vacuum that fanned the flames for the weed of terrorism to sprout into a worldwide scourge. Beware of the liberal mind and its fiery conscience. Those familiar with the beer hall putsch must remember when der Fuhrer delivered his rant against Jews and Roman Catholics. Our mini reformer will begin his career with a simple beer summit to confront police brutality. In the new rhetoric for change the term bourgeois as the enemy of the working class will simply be referred to as the top one percent millionaires and billionaires. Absent opposites as our guide there was no index for what was lawless and extra constitutional. Even the idea of an opposition party was no threat to a figurehead Caesar who threatened a government shutdown unless his every act was approved. How ironic, for it was he, not them, who would shut it down. There was something sinister and egomaniacal about escalating the debt into the realm of bankruptcy, while at the same time depleting the military at a time of greatest threat. We were living in a transformational cataclysm which produced a whole segment of the society as victimized being the sacrificial lambs of an evil system. This lie has produced mean, hateful weeds to choke off the enforcers of law and order and anything that opposes what made this nation great.

An economic crisis absent freedoms moral response had whole departments of government not only politicized but militated against opposing constituents. Whoever would suspect the IRS would target conservative groups during an election to be singled out for reprimand. Then under Senate investigation prosecution was avoided by taking the 5th amendment and destroying of all e-mail evidence. Again when the Justice Dept. was implicated in the issuing of high powered weapons to drug cartels, without surveillance, of which innocents were killed and one weapon discovered in a Paris terror attack, they swept under the rug. Those were the dark days of a morally sanitized objective knowledge run amuck in corruption. High government officials were able to transmit top secret information from a home installed personal server, then lie to Congress after thousands of e-mails again were destroyed without reprimand. Although blatantly condemned by the FBI and exonerated by the Justice Dept. of all guilt, half the population of like carnivore may weasel her name into the nation's highest office.

Our worst political strategy of the new Adonis will be the dishonorable ploy to reach out to hells earthly terror state with the olive leaf impeachable gesture to unfreeze billions in assets paving the way for development of the nuclear bomb. Never did I envision a nation founded on the principles of a Christian morality sign a pact with the author of hells confusion of lies. Especially a demonic state that rails daily from the scorner's seat: death to America and death to Israel our greatest ally. We were witnessing a revival of the witchcraft vial weed to choke off all remnant of the Judeo-Christian epoch. What these scoundrels lacked of essential wisdom was the truth of prophesy which atones the soul in word of law that I will paraphrase as; "they who bring curse upon Israel, I will send primal damnation to round that land." So beloved rejoice in the belief that it is not economic depravity that closed the once blessed door of Eden II. To be ignorant of natural law as the governance over a divine miracle of creative opposites is an eternal blemish leading to the demise of Gods proudest Eden II.

Never again will another nation be bestowed the honor to tame hells adversary so that nation shall not lift up sword against nation, neither shall they learn war anymore. If pure freedom could unite a figment of charred matter to an equal portion of spirit essence and create indescribable cynosure perfection, was it not possible for man to harness it to curb his every ill, only if we first bond in unity its evil adversary.

When Christianity first made its debut in the new world the opposing weed of witchcraft appeared to choke its presence. Liberal historians were quick to defame Christianity to create a false judgement against freedoms co-equal. With one foot in hell and the other guarding the liberal totem of science, make feast of the following folly they wrought by untying the Gordian knot of hell with the universal lie.

A. By evolution which is neither a law nor a force they will annul the natural laws of creation for the civil and corruptible of man.

B. Duality which confirms a heaven and hell unity will be invalidate as knowledge.

C. The word God and associated prayer, bible readings and symbols will be expunged from the classroom and "Big Bang" extolled as his heir apparent.

D. Heavens total encyclopedic of pure nonobjective language like beauty, truth, love, life, water, air, fire, electron, atom, etc. that gave all things of matter their character and potential will be confiscated and adulterated as belonging to matter.

E. In order to destroy God, Christianity as the essence of freedom and of God, must be revoked of its virtuous moral precepts of life beginning at conception, marriage as between a man and a woman, and relaxing of gender discriminatory practices.

F. This will lead to the repeal of all state wide abortion laws and a violation of the sacred birthing womb where at present 1.3 million infants are sacrificed in God's eyes to the pagan deity Moloch.

G. None of this was possible if the electron spirit wave responsible for the electro-magnetic generator of all earthly phenomena had not been declared a mater particle. One day we would learn that it was the negative charged electron as the nursemaid of God that made His presence in each of us. Although it is the spirit electron wave that is responsible for light the existential atheist had no choice but to claim light as caused by matter particles bombarding one another. If this were true creation would have disappeared by now.

H. As further insult to God the marble hearted villains had no choice but to refer to the worldwide reserves of portable mineralized energy and building material deposits as fossil fuels specially placed by diastrophism for man's secondary means of progress.

I. And should we not expect the supercilious lie to claim sovereignty over the forbidden realm of climate change as another insult to the most perfect filtration system of supernatural incomprehensible eternal design. The real problem, if truth be known, was not global warming but global mourning and mortification of sorrow for one He created in His image.

J. That mortification extends to the icon of an evolutionary science whose hatred for God would annul the only number in creation willed to man as proof positive of a dual positive and negative matter and spirit unified creation.

EDUCATION

hat should have been the bedrock of an Eden II freedom inspired miracle has instead become the world's most opulent cesspool. Never can we be forgiven by our founders for allowing the most vile weeds of freedom to destroy our traditional beliefs. Without a Plato or Saint Augustine to stand guard over freedoms learning threshold the liberal existential weed was allowed trespass to poison the mind of youth. By what yardstick did we believe that America was invulnerable to every perversion of hells demon of the dust. Should we wonder why an economy is in shamble, when hundreds and thousands of Gods most fertile farmland under the power of eminent domain was confiscated to build opulent structures that today sterilize millions of beautiful mind of our traditional beliefs? How under heavens council did we allow professorships and courses that sought to deride our faithful founders and the greatest economic and political system the world would ever know?

Thousands of busses daily transport millions of students to ethic less immuring chambers never to hear of our greatness in the words God, soul, faith, natural law, pure freedom, duality, the electron wave, electro-magnetic phenomena or the absolute. Today we're becoming immune to police being murdered, terrorism as a plague of humanity, drug use and a million plus abortions a year. No white glove test admits that one in four of our children consider suicide and many are attracted to communist principles that lead to tyranny – the enemy of freedom. When I started this book I used the word zoomorphic to associate man with the animal, and now I regret the insult to the animal, which I have learned to value and thank God daily for what no man or object can equal. I say this because reflecting back to Columbine Newtown and that beautiful Amish school where innocent lives were lost to become haunting memories, not one finger was pointed at our failing schools. By proselytizing the word "quality" which has become their hallmark of liberal lie is a subjective word not applicable to the object.

Aligned to the travesty of education is the liberal opposition, whose point man ascends the helm, to reform the peoples God given rights by ruthless decimation of the blessed constitution. Anyone who aspires to mock or reform that time tested immortal document, unless suckled by wolves, as with Romulus, the founder of Rome, his cause was sinister of reason. A lot had to do with his circuitous route out of Africa where the best schools America had to offer catapult him to the highest office in the land. Somewhere enroute a poisonous rhetoric fueled a vengeance for the paradigm he should have revered. After seven years we can only surmise that his matriculated aspirations were inclined towards hells dregs of a matter over mind socialist ideology. Only a pompous fool saw America's problem as the need for a Marxist makeover. The real need was for a backbone bums-rush of the liberal existential misfits whose progressive warp had short circuit an incentivized freedom. This great American colossus was not in free-fall due to the lack of a central Leviathans disbursement of "free" things and who view God through the serpents tooth. Pity the wretches who removed prayer, bible reading and ignored teaching the pure subjective knowledge of non-matter descriptive quality. No course because of factual description was structured around the subjective essence of words like truth, beauty, love, life, light, gravity, freedom, electro-magnetism, soul, faith, electricity, positive, negative, absolute one, etc. Had the generations been instructed on the power of God's word never would the unflattering lie have become the ploughshare of the naked heart. The lie held back the blush that referred to the dread of terrorism as a J.V. team, or made the comparison that more people are killed in bathtub falls then by terror. And when they did strike it was called "work place violence: or overseas contingency never mentioning the cause as Islamic terrorism. Most troubling was a justice oriented thought police who referred a third grade student to social services for serving "brownies" at school, because it was considered a P.C. racial comment. Never was the racial divide more pronounced under this effete brigand who regarded republicans and Christians as terrorists. Although a silent transformation had the liberal tentacles in every aspect of a nation's lives they rail against slavery yet the cities they govern are like modern plantations rife in poverty, crime, unemployment and young people without self-esteem. These transformers were matter over mind vile jesters with no soul. Their secret to wean the ignorant masses was not with cake but with food stamps, birth control and the erection pill sprinkled with the lie of free health care. The real question was whether in this the most crucial election of our time, could we dissect these thieves of liberty without the shield of freedom as our guide.

Most of us sensed of an approaching storm much like President Kennedy before his trip to Dallas who made note while on the phone; "I see the storm approaching and if it should come I am ready". For we that still remain time remains to right the ship. Let us begin with the word that exists for the sake of the object and again implore the word that sent us to purge the demon in politics and in education. No longer should we base a child's performance on the ability to memorize the abstract quantifying sludge of inert matter without its subjective opposite. To walk into any English class and hear a teacher describe the objective predicate and its subjective quality in purely objective terms was troubling. How could a nation blessed by freedom as the essence of pure quality, be eliminated, as the primary qualifier of the objects character, personality and potential. Unless we can undergird education K thru U with the only absolute that explains all creative things in both positive and negative unity of oneness the whole process of rote memory is not worth a fiddler's dam. This is the transformation we need and unless we extinguish the liberal existential unilinear evolutionary hogwash we should close the ethic less chambers and pay off the generational debt we've burdened our offspring with.

When the masterminds of the dust destroyed duality, heaven and hell became a united root that made no distinction between good and evil. The past and the future became the now. Within a half century, to their ignorance, the balance wheel of creation called conflict, as man's greatest challenge, escaped its bond with freedom. Absent an ethic and the knowledge of truth the liberal existentialist ascended Gods second Eden under the egis that economic inequality was the culprit of national discord. The creation was purposely conceived out of opposites as proof that nothing could ever be equal except in opportunity and in death. Bear in mind that in matter there is no truth of anything, neither in its language or its mathematics which were conceived in the imperfect state of hell. Just because objective fact can diagnose the things of matter to reveal the nature of the essence that gave it word or number, never can it observe the cause of its origin. This was Gods way of protecting the pure of essence from adulteration by man.

If transformation is a problem then first begin by purging the rot that infects the most perfectly designed system on the face of earth. That antidote is not to invest government as the enemy of freedom with the power to redistribute the wealth. Look at what they've done in just seven years by turning earned success into learned helplessness with crippling debt. Their attack on the successful risk takers has produced a multi-cultural mobocracy such as occupy wall street, code pink, black lives matter, Laraza and others. Even more dangerous is their use of civil law to redefine what life is and when it begins by hells standard. For the true liberal existential matter over mind, chicken before the egg progressive, their hierarchy of loyalty begins with self then party and government. Men of faith place God before country and self.

The fact that we were nestled between two divergent worlds one of object and another of primal subject was no reason to obliterate the perfect for the defective. Few are alive to remember that as early as the 17th century all education centered on the old Satan deluder act. It was all about the good, the true and the beautiful of scripture. A wonderful prelude to Gods freedom inspired Judeo-Christian Eden II. They glorified the past with its uplifting word unlike today where we abhor that which spawn greatness and educate for the future of which no fact can reveal what is to come. Today we are left with the stress of not knowing anything for certain. So we turn to government which is akin to the witchcraft weed of communism that surfaced to choke the essence of the word. Having replaced faith for fact and the traditional of belief for the liberal existential of government, they control the word and they become the God of land, its industry, energy, trade, mining, health care, climate, food production, police, pharmaceutical, bathroom use, child rearing, abortions, birth control, etc.

Never will a child hear the terms subjective essence unless he smells its aroma from the majestic flower or tastes it in its fermented state. When Pasteur discovered alcohol he thought it was the essence of life. Nowhere does education focus attention to the vital soul, as the essence of excellence that motivates the inert matter embryo to its numbered DNA potential. Instead, they worship the demon of government as their benefactor. The American inventive genius and miracle of a freedom liberating essence is unlike what any government agency could ever emulate. The time has come to ask, "My God, my God, why have we forsaken thee".

TEA PARTY – PATRIOT OR VILLAIN?

*F*or society, tea is a soothing beverage but in freedoms eyes it converts to a subjective acronym meaning, "Tyranny Expulsion Agent." No greater enemy of freedom exists on earth like the germ of an authoritarian oppressor of the free will. How soon we lose sight of the TEA PARTY namesake, sifted by God to expel a foreign tyrant, imperative for the safe launching of his second Eden America. Now barely two centuries later they are again solicited by the invincible one to expel a homegrown licentious prototype that threatens the Constitutional lifeblood of that divine covenant. The peril we face is a stark reminder of how great the animus for God has evolved since the demon of the dust challenged him in Eden one. Since then truth has been replaced with psychology and creation with a junk "Big Bang" science aided by the quazi-pagan university and its mind altering elixir to expunge everything that remotely advances Christianity. Beginning with the 15th century Renaissance the assault by a mimetic science has ascended Big Bang to the throne on high and sealed the heavens except for futile experiments and false hypotheses. To claim the culprit as science is a misnomer for there is no such thing. There are only sciences that cover every facet of a culture. This one called "applied" has assumed the responsibility for explaining creation to man. Although hampered by freedoms wise decision to deny an imposter the factual knowledge of creative truth will not hinder the demons of false eminence from seeking notoriety through other abstruse minds. Their trinity of Darwin, Freud and Marx coupled to Nietzsche's anti-religious rants, when transmute to economics, psychology and natural selection will empower the liberal professorships to construct an altar to an objective material god. What better catalyst was there to erase ones inner world of faith so the power grubbing tyrant can rule through devilish deed. And none was more devilish and earth shattering than under false pretense to preach "equality" for the masses through redistribution of capitalist wealth. Had Karl Marx the architect of redistribution and his modern idols been educated to the only absolute willed to man they would know that nothing of a positive and negative electro-magnetic creation is equal nor can anything ever be. The one caveat is that we are all equal in death and in the conflict arising from a creation cast from the opposing unequals of a heaven and earth unity. The adage that all men are created equal only means being born without class or rank. God was masterful in creating a universe out of diametric unequals whose reality in the human sphere causes conflict of chaos with the need not for equality but for the challenge to apply ones talents to overcome conflict through the blessings of freedom. Christianity provides the ethic for which a reward and not a punishment is provided from conflict.

Only those of a perverted anti-God existential view that man and matter account for all reality foster the idea of equality to make themselves superior. Once inferiors become superior they become revolutionaries. Karl Marx the atheist revolutionary of equal distribution as the solution for creative conflict was an enemy of freedom and of Christianity. The best proof that inequality of difference is the norm one has to but realize that without the unequal extremes of plus and minus one there would be no balance, no perpetual motion, no wind or current to distribute heat and cold or gravity to attract the electron generative wave. No atom of proton and electron which means there would be no creation of anything. It is inequality of difference that gives us beauty, the propagative atom seed for love, life and the beauty caused by unlikes. If equality was the norm there would be no winners or losers, no challenge to work and excel and most of all there would be an absence of conflict which challenges one to live and not wantonly die out. As the master once wisely stated, "the poor will always be with us." Tolstoy explained it by stating, "The more that is given the less the people will work for themselves, and the less they work, the more their poverty increases." Let us not forget that ever since President Johnson declared a war on poverty untold billions have been spent on equality only to prove the problem has not abated, it has exponentially metastasize.

America will aspire to a Golden Age not because of government motivating some to lean on those who lift, but because of limiting the tyrant of government from interfering by regulation, taxation and stimulation that retards the freedom to pursue opportunity. The bountiful resources of the world were not made to be regulated, taxed, supervised or equally distributed by bureaucratic demons who believe they are the self-righteous heirs of heaven. Strange indeed that Gods second Eden enlightenment of unrivaled power, progress and inventive freedom now withers before an immoral caretaker equality that has lost favor with God. The trepidation that is upon the land has caused few to reflect on Dostoyevsky who warned, "That tyranny is a habit capable of being developed, and at last becomes a disease." That disease which now festers is because the Christian virtues that promulgate an incentivized freedom have been abysmally aborted. Yet, who today believes that freedom is not of man but was first breathed by God to stem the fiery first stage of an unorganized positive numbered protogenic matter in abnormal association with positive fiery hell. Two positives do not make a super positive. They will repel in a state of convulsive anarchy. Was God setting a precedent for shunning "equals" as a part of civil law? And is this why man will be breathed by God of negative charge while woman is cast from the positive rib of man to satisfy unequal opposites in unity of one? This does not mean that negative is good and positive is bad. Both words are cast from the word of one to open creation to unfathomed timeless dimension and allow an absentee landlord to maintain custody through challenge and response of inequality. Freedom was born to retard chaos not to make compromise with it as a child is taught. In times of peril and saturated by the dross of ignorance and bureaucratic slag freedom again intervenes in the midst of a maturing ochlocracy of tyrannical rule. Having watched his word extinguished and commandments laid waste, one last appeal is to his most adored vessel for love and life from whom her positive seed the creation was planned. No one has suffered more to a perverted freedom that saw her sons die in vain to an objective freedom laced with sin, or to watch as her unborn were sacrificed by the millions to the false deity Moloch. Today her beautiful body has become the amenage for the erotica transport across freedoms sacred ionizing wave into every home and handheld touchpad.

Then in roguish perview the demons of a licentious democracy appear to grace our living quarters as applause seeking, freedom flattering, truth perverted champions of the people. Unfortunately the freedom they espouse has been severely lacerated and the people once idolized as American have long since been lobotomized.

Such is the reason for freedoms unveiling of this long annulled mind piercing, lifesaving, tyranny shattering, ignorance repelling symbol of the only "absolute" willed to man. It appears to eradicate and globally extricate the libertine envenimous demigod of the dust. When this clay miner's son of a saintly mother was privileged to discover what Einstein failed to do my first thought was to have it cast in jewelry. Soon after its display I realized that not one plebeian in a hundred knew what an absolute was and when told cared less. That's when the eureka moment struck, and instead of running naked through the streets shouting as Archimedes did, "I found it." I saw it as the Holy Grail scepter for God's secret army to save freedom from passing into darkness. Having lived through Americas Golden Age and knowing that freedom is the spirit of God and Christianity the essence of freedom everything about this miraculous symbol appeared to speak. Similar to standing beside the famed Liberty Bell and watching my students gaze at its ominous scar while hearing that it was caused by brittleness from an admixture of alloys. I often wondered what if the bell could speak, as it often did in times past, would it state that not one bell in over four hundred years of casting by the famous White chapel foundry ever cracked and most still operate today. Per chance would the bell state that it was not brittleness of the metal but was a reminder to the generations of a brittleness of an unfaithful trustee of freedom. Not only does the mighty force of freedom speak in signs and symbols but for me to the subconscious when the matter molecules have retired for needed rest.

In order to destroy God, the demon of the dust must confiscate and adulterate a pure subjective language that gives all things of inert matter unique character, personality and potential including the electron spirit wave that energizes a total creation. What they failed to realize is that matter conceived in fire is not only inert but has no ideal above its fiery genesis. Therefore, if God did not exist as an ideal, the demons at a loss to find anything perfect would of necessity need to invent a prototype. Fortunately, for a world in turmoil there comes ironclad proof that a heavenly God does exist. From the miraculous symbol it appears as the only absolute truth willed to man. It comes at a time when science now admits of knowing less about creative truth than when Socrates invented the germ of science twenty five hundred years ago.

Cast your eye to the central axis representing absolute one as the only number in creation able to bond to one side the symbol for positive earth whose essence is gravity, and directly opposite the negative sign that retracts into the pure ethereal realm of spirit essence. No thought gives rise on the sentient mind unless programmed to these two fascinating dual forces of positive and negative one. Opposites were man's only means for knowing that anything exists. Only an invincible intellect could design such a means to inspire the subtlety of conflict as a universal challenge to make a stable and secure future by the restraining action of freedom. God's second Eden will become the most productive and revered because of the restraining ethic of a freedom inspired Christianity. Now as the Judea Christian ethic dies and freedom fades into oblivion the culture is in moral collapse. Without opposites there would be no balance, no perpetual motion, no light and darkness, no wind or current to make fresh and pure or an invincible atom to construct an earth, air, fire and water completeness. Absent Earth and sky and diadem of heavenly jewel to adore the face of mother earth, all would be bleak and deathless. The most damning hew leveled at the heart of God's second Eden was the demigods wedge that split the absolute at its core. In Eden one the chiding viper enticed the woman to eat of the forbidden fruit of the tree of knowledge. Eden two will see the entire knowledge of the tree of good confiscated and ravaged. A total encyclopedia of supernormal qualifying spiritual knowledge will be absconded like beauty, truth, love, life, freedom, virtue courage, honor, mother, father, child, light, soul, mathematics, science, marriage, gravity, electricity, conscience, prayer, color, earth, air, fire, water, etc. If we single out freedom which was breathed by God to stem fiery chaos and convert its purity to make mutual concession with evil is to blight the tree of liberty. A tree which Jefferson claimed was watered by the blood of patriots and which for America made it a sacred symbol.

Beware that freedom knows itself as the spirit of God which is impervious to desecration. When freedom was pure God's second Eden united in faith was kept secure from the powers of darkness. When the demon of the dust converted pure freedom into an objective prototype they will destroy the fabric on a once virtuous nation and suffer loss of the protective shield of freedom. For when freedom dies the evil spore of terror fills its sacred vacuum. Following the zenith of Athenian glory and absent a divine philosophy an opposing weed of barbarism will bring decay and depravity. Because we don't learn from history our nemesis is the weed of terrorism whose wailing destruction blazons because freedoms defensive shield is severed of moral unity. The tragedy of God's second Eden revolves around the word unity whose persecution has unleashed the conflict of fiery chaos to destroy the culture. Absent the unity of positive and negative difference the result in simple logic is the creation of a "short circuit" breach between sense and essence making us abandoned fugitives of freedom. In real life not one war, and there have been four since the great one fought for freedom, that has ended short of a stalemate or defeat. This should provoke concern as to why fifteen terrorists could enter the country with fake passports, open bank accounts, enter flight school with the desire to steer, not fly a plane, the rain fire from the sky killing thousands. A marred super power patina left few wondering if we had lost freedoms protective shield of faith. In a dual creation of dual language never did any course offer dual interpretations for words like freedom, language, mathematics, creation, man, electricity, gravity, morality, truth, justice, fact vs faith, etc. Eden two will in the prime of paradise forfeit its soul by replacing faith for fact which because it was conceived in fire was denied all access to truth. This would compel science to rely on "probability" as the assumed model for truth. They had no choice but to explain light as being caused by matter particles bombarding one another which was ludicrous. The negative electron wave will be called a positron meaning a matter particle morphed of its structure as if to say is was bi-sexual. Because of imperfect fact they must claim man as the animal and inventor of knowledge math and science including the ellipse, freedom, and big bang as an evolved creation absent a beginning. For those who harbor skepticism with the word God try as a substitute the word "unity." Unity means state of being one and whole. "In the beginning was the word and the word was one in unity with God; John 1:1." Only by divine miracle are the two most important extremes of positive object and negative spirit bond in the wholeness and completeness of a divine unity. Only man because of his free will exemption must rely on the power of freedom to bond him in oneness with creation. Some of us carry the number that interfaces with freedom others must be educated to its motivation. Unity as a principle of higher math, although never taught, simply means that in a world of competing opposites one side must imbibe and take custody of the other as with heaven over earth, water over land and air over fire. To replace unity, which for most cases requires the word "no" instead of the compromising opposite of yes is the secret to success.

The beauty of this symbol of the absolute readily implies that the negative pure must assume moral custody over the corruptible of matter. Only through a freedom inspired faith does the illusion of doubt and mystery fade into a oneness of truth.

Big bang was only the transmuted first stage of a positive charged protogenic unorganized number bond to that of a positive charged fire to provoke a convulsing state of hell to stand opposite the pure of negative essence. This beginning would satisfy the absolute of a heaven and hell extreme difference in need of unity. That unity is not possible until the word "free" is breathed by the word of one to stem the inferno. At this juncture there is no water, air, electron, atom, light or vital soul. After freedom is pronounced and the convulsing restrained, stage two begins with God's implanting of the vital soul and the electrons presence for the construction of the starter seed miracle atom. Every atom will be composed of two anti-atoms whose density escapes all detection as they retract into the word of positive and negative one. J. D. Jukes in his book *Man Made Sun* states that one hundred million atoms could be placed side by side along the outer edge of a postage stamp. And if every atom is composed of a proton and electron anti-atom their density as being the word itself is nothing short of a miracle.

For those who find the word God hard to perceive consider that all things of creation have their beginning in one starter positive and negative seed. That seed propagate to one hundred and seven known offspring must then pollinate individually and cross pollinate into a ubiquitous variety of an immune perfection.

Our epiphenomenal secondary universe will rightfully be created out of chaos and patterned on the embryonic seed of the mother in unity with the negative essence of God. This fact alone should make man forever vigilant of retraining chaos through an incentivized freedom that never abrogates that right to an authoritarian master. The following is proof that only through faith and not fact truth is self-evident. One proton of matter unified to one of essence will create the offspring known as hydrogen. It will be the first, lightest and most abundant of all elements. The first mission of hydrogen will be to extend the new heaven to infinity which according to Cambridge University is still ongoing. After the maturation of eight anti-atom protons with eight of essence the element oxygen is born. Only the creator can combine hydrogen two parts to one of oxygen in creating the staff of life water. Imagine a child being taught that water occurred when big bang cooled when in truth in stage one there were no atoms, no water, no air, no electron, no light and only nothingness until the word "free" restrains the erratic craving of a soul. By facts we only know that something exists but not of the essence that gave it existence. They can tell us that hydrogen and oxygen form water but only God knows the essence of number that formed hydrogen, oxygen or water. They can explain the ocean basins factually but not their carving or how the bottoms were lined with a magnesium base to withstand the tremendous pressure of its buoyancy. Faith takes one into the negative universe of truth where no fact can go. Faith tells us that to insure perfect balance two troughs were necessary and the excess material cast upward to become a majestic regent of the sky. Facts make their presence in things that grow old and atrophy while faith reveals the presence of things not seen which are eternal and everlasting. The demon of the dust represents the occasion for spreading of the muck and not the cause from which it was conceived in fire.

That wonderful constant of air will be transmute from the major gasses of nitrogen and oxygen along with numerous others and amazingly become the guardian over the constant of fire. When human life is created it will be composed of 95% of hydrogen, oxygen and nitrogen in union with positive charged carbon. Three negative conductors for ionization of the vital soul to become custodian over an infirmed positive body. Should we wonder why this age is obsessed over health care caused by a short circuit full of doubt, illusion, stress, misery and faithless ignorance? In the physical world every electron generated digital device requires a "plug in" charger as an energy source. However, the human body is not equipped for such an external device, and aside from food for energy, it has no way of inspiring the electron nursemaid to charge the freedom loving soul to transcend in oneness with the most feeble of body. Our system for spiritual ionization is by the simple password "I believe" set to a vocalized flow of fervent prayerful atoms which is the most profound form of education.

When Sigmund Freud professed neurosis of the mind as the cause of conflict, and which our schools adopted by teaching the need for releasing ones pent-up inhibitions, what he was really prescribing was how to become alienated from freedom and pawns of chaos. The pleasure of things of the flesh makes us proud before they devour us. We know good and evil exist but only faith can balance and unify the two. Remember that modern medicine prescribes hundreds of timely remedies – God prescribes but one.

Just because no mind of man could explain negative electicety, the atom, hydrogen, oxygen, nitrogen, carbon, water, earth, air, fire, soul or the remaining 103 elements and their creation was no reason to follow the Marxist adage "if it can't be explained create a substitute or erase it from reason." As I have proven from the absolute all things can be explained through the faith of negative one not by fact which has its origin in an objective state of hell.

That brings us to the reality of an unfaithful trustee of freedom who has neutered God, disavowed unity, abandoned the soul, bisects the creation and confiscated and adulterated its pure subjective language. This will allow freedom to make compromise with evil unleashing a short circuit demon of the dust to bring disgrace to God's second Eden causing freedom to exit the land. In this majestic world of opposites, signs often foretell of proceeding events. Summertime convection ascending to do combat with the negative charged colder air often breaks the silence with the crash of thunder and torrential downpours. The result can lead to power outages, down lines, blown transformers and with the likes of tornadoes wreak havoc. Cannot a similar comparison be made between the dueling corruptible of ideology and the transforming soul of freedom.

When the election of 2008 ushered in what the pundits called an economic tsunami all attention focused on the mundane of man as responsible for the near collapse. The short circuit echo-chambers saw the trepidation as caused by the superficial of easy credit, lack of financial regulation, mortgages without collateral, worthless derivatives, mounting debt, venture capitalism, discretionary spending and Ponzi schemes of corruption. In freedoms eyes all of this was a non-sequitor "probability." No genius saw the near collapse through the lens of freedom and the moral glue that once mold a polyglot people in Godly unity. 2009 brought a young firebrand to the helm with the oratorical bravado of a Daniel Webster and ideological brashness of Adolph Schicklgruber. When he spoke chills went up the legs of some echo-chamber effete. In advance of his coronation a delirium tremens had settled over the land causing many to wonder if this was the pilot to mitigate the storm. The first billow of dismay came from the plummer to whom the new Adonis expressed his desire to redistribute the wealth. Soon after, the same impression made by his better half caused another political satirist to express the wish: "I hope he fails." I would be remiss not to suggest that freedom likewise was using an advance omen of portending concern.

Within days of the immaculation a disguised hope and change of the culture appeared eminent when likeminded czars and liberal Praetorian Guard began descending from the Trojan horse. However, one inadvertent caveat stood in the way. For in order to dismantle the worlds greatest freedom inspired market oriented individual incentivized system, they first had to pull asunder the residual spirit that sustained it. These wrecking balls nurtured on the ideology of a "God is dead" generation were ignorant of their instructor's low bred allegiance to the Marxist model, divorced from a higher ideal that shapes and regulates all things. None the less, he must avoid the mistakes of a distant ideolog and revolutionary whose conversion of a culture began by nationalizing the agricultural sector creating widespread revolts. This oligarch would use a more deceptive approach by using "equality" as the underlying theme in concert with party bribes, strong arm tactics, kickbacks, paybacks, cornhusker deals, outright lies and under the cover of Christmas railroad through Congress a nationalized health care plan without one republican vote. With the stroke of a pen one sixth of the American economy and greatest health care system in the world was turned over to bureaucrats. This began the first stage death of capitalism to a freedom destroying leviathan who never produced anything but regulation and control and until now never effectively able to run a post office. Compounding the problem was the largest bailout of stimulus in American history that gave the debt suzerainty over the nation's death. Much of it went to green energy that was all green and no energy, shovel ready jobs without any shovels, banks that refused to loan and bankrupt companies to sugar coat union pensions.

As if a plaque descended on the land everyday seemed reminiscent of ancient Egypt. To list those that scandalized the lawless health care fiasco would be indescribable and unbelievable. On the global front a tinderbox of terror and aggression was filling the vacuum of the worlds once most respected superpower. At home a praying mantis style blight of thousands of children began crossing the porous southern border overwhelming the system. At first glance one had to ruminate that this was freedoms recompense for the suffering millions never given a chance outside the sacred womb. Freedom had to be arbiter where stolid demigods of matter extolled a self-righteous superiority of divine right denied any man. To claim lordship over health care was one thing but to supersede God in control over weather and climate was ludicrous. By heavens standard earth knows no desecration. She smells regeneration from the timely rhythms of death, decay and yes pollution. For any tyrant to believe they, by regulating the blessed CO_2 invisible gas, that is monitored by the greatest filtrating miracle of

God to intercept incoming harmful cosmic rays as well as manmade pollutants ascending upward was an act of lunacy. No Virginia, man in not a regulator of weather, climate or of the majestic jet stream high above earth that controls all weather patterns below. The sensible way to control the forces of nature is to unshackle the metamorphosed soul to seek unity for a divine protection from the distraught caretaker elements monitored by freedom. What these demigods referred to as fossil fuels when big bang belched and the mountains heaved, trapping an ocean full of marine life that was converted into coal, oil and gas was another hoax. The truth is that on every continent as part of Gods dowry abundant mineral and carbon deposits were placed in reserve for man's secondary means for energy and progress. Because inert matter gave the revolutionaries little to bloviate over, why not as a crowd pleaser, latch onto the invincible CO_2 which plants need to grow and reproduce into oxygen so man can breathe in order to live. After all if they could usurp the reserved power clause of the states why not the invisible CO2 whose many causes come from respiration, combustion, distillation, fermentation, condensation and innumerable sources that surely need regulation and control as it relates to wealth. Isn't it time to reverse the baneful practice of these intractables from control over education, immigration, poverty, equality, trade, finance, autos, voting rights, welfare, health, food stamps, social security disability, energy, mining, climate, surveillance, and cornering of hollow point shells. In record time the list has expanded to include gun sales, light bulbs, toilets, café standards, census, welfare, school lunches, student loans, abortion, marriage, minimum wage, right to work, trafficking of guns, surveillance of conservative groups and supposed protectors of women to oppose the false war on this helpless creature. Of grave concern is to ask whether our demon of the dust schools have dumbed down the populous enough so that in concert with a welfare state the uphill climb is too great to overcome a Tea Party revolution. While massive printing of unbacked fiat hovered over the health of the iconic stock market, jobs and production were mired on a sand bar. The debt continued to escalate into hyper ventilated territory ignoring the wisdom to cut taxes, balance the budget and drastically cut government spending. Unfortunately, none of this fit the Marxist model. In disarray and insulated inside their Teflon coated Machiavellian cocoon, the urgency became that of all tyrants to shame and blame the opposition and the burning Bush. As stimulus refused to stimulate, and green energy turned to wasted soot, runaway debt turned everything the monarch touched to the plaque of rust. A blatant withdraw from fledgling democracies where the nation's blood and treasure was sacrificed, without a stabilizing contingency, was beyond rebuke. There was no rationale to explain why the downsizing of our military, when the threat of terrorism was of grave concern and the main function of the government was to defend the country from foreign enemies. Then there was the reading of Miranda rights to the enemies of freedom while setting free the worst of the worst to strike again. And should they and their ilk not grimace at the greatest insult against freedom by presidential approval of abortion, free contraceptives and same sex marriage. Or by declaring the revered Constitution as too negative in what it limits a government from doing. Surely the complaint is because this sacred lamp of liberty is what was covenant with

God to restrain the scoundrel from shredding individual liberty. This is reason why for the first time ever a president has found reason to apologize for American greatness. By apologizing for Americas greatness is to insult freedom and its spirit of God. What form of haughty iconoclast can apologize for an American creative genius and marvel of a capitalist market economy that awakened the sleeping giant and Russian bear who taunt the holy ground they now emulate. Who was this monarch of the IRS that blatantly censured conservative groups that may have impacted his re-election? And by whose command did the NSA secretly monitor phone conversations by ignoring the freedom of speech. One scandal that baffles the imagination is why weapons were made available to the Mexican drug cartels absent any tracking and were responsible for the killing of a border guard and numerous others. Then as if by divine right Congress was not informed of any of these illicit acts of malfeasance and when they were censored responded by condemning the fault finders of phony accusations. From Tolstoy comes the definition of the most hardened and repulsive form of conceit. He states that "those who claim to know nothing, and absolve themselves from all blame, possess the truth of a science of their own invention, which to them is absolute truth." Because this article reveals the only absolute truth there is need to revise Tolstoy's definition of conceit to read: "those who claim to know nothing and absolve themselves from all blame, possess the truth of a science of their own invention, which in truth is an absolute lie." Had they sensed a moral breach between the corruptible of man and the founder's divine covenant the ship of faith may not have list off center. Prior to passing of the torch freedom did not read the tea leaves to know what was about to be unleashed from under the immoral rock. Godly wisdom had long since warned not to sacrifice his precious offspring to the false deity Moloch, yet shuttered at what was destined to be. This emaculation was the first maculated inauguration of Eden II in which the venomous condoning of the profane act would be sanctioned. Associated to the travesty was an authoritarian carnage to destroy the core of an incentivized labor for a nationalized and redistributive demon of the dust model. Freedom saw in advance a shredding of the sacred commandments enshrined in the worlds most revered constitution that respect life, love, marriage, beauty, truth, virtue and motherhood. In Eden one Adam and Eve and the animals were banished past the flaming sword of cherub. Eden II saw the reverse where freedom would banish leaving behind the scourge of a terror plagued anarchical hell.

Therefore, no other reason exists why in its final glory freedom must interpose a miracle to sift from the living soil in 2010 a devoted Tea Party faithful whose instinct was to purge and purify the once esteemed house of the people. They appeared as a silent and sacred reawakening to the espoused offspring of Eden's christening. Their purging of the House was so astronomical that immediate outrage exploded from the highest reaches of the short circuit political lair. Realizing their power was threatened brought an envenimous testicular outrage exhibiting their mentor's response to recoil and viciously attack. The tepid emissaries of freedom would be labeled as Nazi, racist, terrorist, enemies of the poor, the middle class, of women, green energy, climate change, equality and immigration. They were called Astroturf, homophobes, anarchists, tyrants and supporters of millionaires and billionaires. Quite a contrast to the honest patriotic defenders of the Bill of Rights who only wanted smaller government, a strong military, balanced budgets, lower taxes, border protection, a sacred ballot, anti-redistribution policies, anti-nationalization of health care and an end to crony capitalism and runaway entitlements. They were upset over the monstrous debt, the Federal Reserve's printing of unbacked fiat, failure of the executive branch to abide by the check and balance system and a growing authoritarian subjugation of the free enterprise system.

During this unsettled state of an alien ideology at home and a mounting terrorism abroad the spirit of freedom was not idle nor was the ghosts of Rome from peering in. As an impending blight settled over the tree of liberty every act promulgated by the ruling demon of the dust and ignored by the praetorian press was fraught with the plaque of scandal and cover-up. Reminiscent of the plaques of Egypt these were subtle warnings that freedom was not only wiser than the pen and phone but command the grist mill for those who sought to wound the spirit and befall the soul. How did the most enviable nation on earth wander off course in believing that freedom the quintessential of ideal thought was an invention of sordid man. And what matter of man concurred in the greatest heist ever by allowing the pure of freedoms essence to become adulterated by the corruptible demons of fiery hell. Even the miraculous ellipse that bond the cusps of one antedates the creation as the plane for setting all cosmic form to perpetual freedom of motion. It is freedom that allows man by faith to transcend where no fact of matter dare go into the negative realm to the footstool of God.

No school in dissemination of objective dross motivates a child to revel on the negative side of absolute one where peace and joy reign. None would envision the atoms interior where the electron nursemaid makes God's presence the mainstay of all creative things. Only when the sense of man is in unity with the essence of freedom is their wholeness of body and soul. It was this lack of effusive quality that prompted the advent of Christ to spend time in admonition leading to the greatest spiritual movement in history. No history lesson focuses on how Christianity brought about Roman demise or saved man from extinction by leading him back to the living soil for basic survival and realignment of the moral soul.

What historians will label as the Dark Ages is superlative in explaining the theory of opposites or duality. By natural law every seed is shadowed by a destructive virtue-less weed. No sooner is the seed of Christianity sown than its opposing anti-God, existential demon of the dust weed aroused to offer combative challenge. Amidst the aftermath of feudal tenure challenged by mercantilism followed by the new city state and the challenge for autocratic power through exploration, discovery, wars and settlement the industrial age is breeding the weed of a material science to challenge the Christian evangels on their way to Gods second Eden.

No one knows the secret of the virtue-less weed that springs up to anonymously oppose the fertile seed. Death is such a weed to accompany the human seed. Freedom had its weed of tyranny that now has its stranglehold. No greater weed was ever sprout to oppose the faith of a Christian idealism based on the seed of an eternal essence. Once God sent his son to jettison the greatest moral movement of faith on the face of earth the weed of naturalism will appear to destroy the supernatural. Its destructive pollen will be vent by the physical, biological, psychological, social and emotional canons of the scientific method of feeble fact. Following the great Christian harvest of the Middle Ages and prior to their long trek to Eden II this opposing weed will leave Italy and head north out of Renaissance. By the prodding of freedom they will veer right out of Germany and head East for the cold steppes of Russia. Here they will instigate a bloody revolution, kill the Czars and institute a policy of nationalization and collectivism. The response will cause wide spread peasant revolts, mass executions, slave labor gulags and Siberian exiles. Blame was placed on the surrounding capitalist countries. This did not dampen the desire to create a communist utopia by equal distribution of production. What follows and which should have been inculcated in the American psyche is their forming of the first international front for the purpose of inciting the proletariat working poor to unite in a world-wide revolution to destroy capitalism and seize the private means of production. Never would they give up on this idea knowing that pure freedom without protective vigilance was as vulnerable to the leach of tyranny as God was to a demented science. While God's second Eden was in its Golden Age, the threat of a world-wide axis tyranny would command for American freedom to unleash its greatest generation, for the preservation of life in the spirit of heavenly valor. As our ally during World War II will be the avowed communist enemy of expressed determination to destroy the American capitalist system. Victory of World War II would end a brutal axis oppression but what it did not end was the malignant spoils of the war and of the enemy that followed freedom home. Beset by an almost sacred jubilation the nation exudes with an immortal quality of invulnerability. We were in for a surprise. On the coattails of victory the avengers saw a panacea for the honorable extensions of civil and human endeavor and for the skullduggery leach of liberty a due process for the dishonorable. Front and center was the pusillanimous stealth of the united front and its communist party USA to form bedfellow with labors disgruntled, the liberal professorships and reactionary press. The Redscare of 1919 resurfaced with claims that communist subversives had ascended the highest reaches of the state department. In 1954 Senate hearings were conducted and broadcast by the invention of television which proved to be groundless in accusation. When I entered teaching in 1959 the threat was still evident as I was asked to take an oath "that I was not now or ever had been a member of the communist party?" The threat was most destructive when it was learned that America's atomic secrets had been passed to the Soviets by the Rosenberg spies allowing them to detonate their first bomb. They would beat us to the punch with the more powerful hydrogen prototype. This would provoke a cold war and a containment policy with communist aggression in Eastern Europe, Korea, Vietnam and the placing of missiles in Cuba ninety miles from our shore.

Under the cloak of secrecy in 1957 the world would awaken to the trepidation of the Soviet launching of "sputnik", the world's first earth orbiting satellite. Caught by surprise as we were on 9-11 the immediate response was to unofficially empower science as the headmaster of American education with its imperative to "catch-up" in the race for space. A more appropriate phrase might be to link-up and assimilate for this was the death of prayer and bible reading and the beginning of a legal conversion of freedom into its objective counterpart. I was there to see the conversion as sex; drugs and rock and roll were just what the Freudian doctors of a Marxist utopia had in mind. The malaise was compounded by the millions of woman many of them mothers who were jarred from the home during the war to fill a vacuum in the work place with unintended consequence. She will be replaced, if not wholly, by an insensate electronic amoral brain for viewing animated images on to the retina of the eye to follow the optic nerve to the brain. Before the war huxters came on Saturday and outside now they took up residence within. Condoms before the war were under the counter and out of view and birth control pills unheard of as were those now offered for an instant erection. Abortion was soon to be made legal to keep pace with instant meals and instant passion. The separation by purgation clause had all but sealed the negative moral and pure universe for the hiatus of an anything goes demon inspired stud farm indoctrination of education. No wonder why in advance of the storm freedom would intervene with another miracle in March of 1953 revealing the most elegant and entrancing divine sculpture ever witnessed of God's handprint in the human gene. This four letter alphabet of dual positive and negative macromolecule revealing ones entire specification of character, personality and potential should have reverberated with heavenly praise until the end of time. Unfortunately, discovery of the celebrated DNA barely made a footnote in science. All it took was when one of its discoverers was asked how he thought it entered the human gene replied; "possible by Aliens." If there was reason for freedom to turn its face and exit the land the time had come. Since that great discovery 95% of the DNA is without purpose while the rest is used mainly in the crime labs. As Eden II fades into the rear view mirror and the conflict of chaos on the march, the one nation bestowed the power to tame it had rightfully fallen into disrepute.

In the physical creation overlooked by science was the constant of chaos as a pillar alongside earth, air, fire and water as a necessary ingredient for the new creation. Only a divine miracle could stem its ferocity by apportioning it in the atoms interior and the remainder placed deep below the crust as a vessel of hell. In the social realm chaos will be apportioned in evil as a means to make strong and shape the spirit of the soul. Only the electron wave could pierce its depth and not become soiled. The same was true of the suns light that passed through the recesses of the dirtiest of pollution and remained pure. Only the restraining power of a freedom inspired Godly faith could tame it. The odyssey of making that happen required sending the son of heaven to walk among us giving testament of word and miracle to enlighten the soul of man. He made the lame walk, the blind see, the leper cleansed, the dead rise, the possessed made clean, the multitudes fed, the thief pardoned and redemption promised beyond the grave. On rising from the dead the greatest spiritual movement in history will transpire. From its blessing the miracle of faith will inspire worldwide cathedrals for the mind to turn fear into courage and doubt into eternal belief. Throughout Europe the might and power of faith still emblazon heaven in masterpieces of bronze and stone, art and music. Mans truest monument will not be by inscription in stone but in a paradise under freedoms watchful eye.

Many of God's miracles while on earth were for the time as well as a postscript for a never ending grandness and admiration to transcend the ages. Unfortunately, powerful opposing demonic spirits aligned to a material idolatry will overtime severely blunt belief in a supreme being. God's second Eden is under such a pall of a quasi-pagan shamanistic netherworld essence of things. In Eden one God planted a miracle garden. Overlooked by a proud people will be the miracle of Eden II as a freedom inspired provisioned plantation blessed with every amenity to foster an earthly paradise. It would not happen without the miracle of beneficent prompting one of which bears example to his pardon of the thief who hung beside him on the cross.

This pardon would not occur at the crucifixion but at the judgment seat of the Father. Broken and crowned with the primal curse and made to wander destitute and in shame beside his wife and mistrusting animal was more than any man could bear. In exile he would see his son kill his own brother and again under countenance of God feel the pain of punishment for another curse and banishment from the ground. Most unusual was the absence of a last name when it was customary for first families to adopt the name of their occupation. Was Adams last name omitted for a special reason or was it too vainglorious for one who was to become a betrayer? In Eden one God was on hand to bless and sanctify all that was good and use the occasion to expose the demon of the dust evil. For the omnificent mind was this to be a trial and error experience that will turn a sinner into a saint or have we forgotten Saul of Tarsus who among the worst of persecutors was made blind before the conversion.

Unlike Eden one its successor would require a faithful evangel to transport the seed for a pre-ordained spiritual harvest. This vanguard was poor as God was poor and sifted like his apostles with the faith to accomplish the impossible. Foremost on the mind of God was the need to prevent freedoms most antagonistic enemy from disrupting his ideal plan. Every civilization of which Toynbee would estimate as twenty three, was short-lived because of authoritarian masters that preyed on the weak. The ledger is replete with tribal leader, caste, slave master, divine right inheritance, those by conquest or by elected mandate as we see today. All are oppressors of individual freedom. Eden II by God's will, must be guaranteed from such domination. No doubt the solution was pre-ordained and part of the master plan that by sign and symbol would one day be revealed.

Only one would be deservedly chosen, made to suffer, pardoned, atoned, redeemed and educated to be the miracle transforming hero for laying the foundation for his second Eden immunization against an oppressive tyrant. As a precedent, the first sign would occur on the cross where before his brutal death he would pardon the thief who hung beside him. When considering the topic of pardon we must not overlook the most penitent man who ever lived saddened by spending every day of his life as a living hell tormented as a traitor to God and to all humanity. Cursed by God and banished past the flaming sword of Cherub alongside his wife and mistrusting animal he would wander in shame a disgraced man. Will this be the one who never given a last name, in a world where all first families acquired the last name of their occupation, was denied for a special occasion or would it be too humiliating to be called Adam Traitor?

While the distant paradise was still struggling to cleanse itself of foreign oppression a young man would enter Oxford University by the name of Adam Smith, on his way to the University of Glasgow, Scotland. Here he will become a renowned professor of logic and moral philosophy never realizing that his preparation was to make him the freedom inspired savior of a second chance redemptive paradise. So far nothing is convincing, certainly not for the demon of a tyrannical dust until the date of 1776 arrives and our founders have just enacted the brilliant Declaration of Independence. Just published and appearing in their hands will be the greatest book ever written on economics and government with an abbreviated title, *The Wealth of Nations* by Adam Smith. Enamored by its principle of Laissez Faire hands off for government was the blueprint for a freedom inspired individual incentivized paradise. Its simple logic proclaimed that by natural law freedom endowed the labor of man and resources of land as the true wealth of a nation absent the long arm of government.

Like the DNA miracle no monument extols the name Adam Smith and no fourth of July celebration conjures a mere remembrance to the mysterious one who provided America a freedom inspired enlightenment. What teacher ever invokes his name to the America doctrine of the invisible hand of competition as the freedom ordained regulator of a supply and demand individual inspired economic system free of government control. In his soul Adam must have envisioned that evil men through greed would find a way to kill competition to avoid the uncertainty of how much to produce and at what price. As before him when they crucified his Christ he must have sensed the same for Laissez Faire giving way to monopolies, trusts, cartels, interlocking directorates and the advent of government regulation. Before his death haunted by Eden one and the fate of Eden II he will order all his manuscripts to be burned.

In summary, this allegory on the absolute will be interpreted by many to have been stylized for the middle ages. I assure you if it were, the pendulum that once registered on the wisdom of God has in this short time been in free fall to an evolved madness fretted by fiery decay. Even to the extent of extolling the shades of Vergil's Aeneid from which Dante adopts its narrative to lead him through hell. How soon the immunity of a hope and change promise fades into a tragedy that merits the clairvoyance of a spiritual and moral enlightenment. The authoritarian autocrats who put us there now turn all hope of redemption to the honorable freedom loving Tea Party faithful to turn the tide in November. It is our only hope to purge the system, reclaim the faith, restore to state government its reserved powers and undergird education with the religious neutral absolute. Science also must form unity with the eternal scientist and all religions relinquish the cloak of vanity for a unity of oneness in the divine precepts of freedom and its immortal constitution. Remember that in this telecommunication age the problem transcends our shores to one of global concern. Place all trust in freedoms pure form and it will guide you. Don't stop short by an election until the clever has castrated the massive expansion of government agencies and their repugnant regulatory power. Finally scrutinize the constitution to find where the executive branch has the delegated power to fundraise and campaign non-stop at tax payer expense. Timed to the malaise overtaking the country is the term illegal. Before casting aspersion let us approach the topic two ways. First to the most auspicious illegal hailed as adjudicator of law and justice of whom many have become the arch trader of freedoms divine Constitutional protections. Sworn to uphold the seven cardinal sins of freedom they have instead legislated to uphold what Benjamin Franklin called the wishes of the scoundrel over Godly wisdom. When Dante divided hell into nine rungs he may have been purporting inauspiciously a separate ledge for each by the presiding number of the court on which they served.

The second illegal is the influx of children who because of porous borders of the unsavory "Dream Act" incentive with political intonation have presented a humanitarian crisis. Most come as Christian and in freedoms eyes may be revenge for the millions aborted in the most inhumane act of nature. Taken one step further this may be freedoms prompting to begin de-centralized control placing more responsibility on the states to seal the border with the National Guard. In the interim take immigration out of the autocrats control urging the churches to screen, house and educate for what may be a blessing. Finally as 1917 approaches and America appears in a fast sprint to pay redistributive honors, cast attention instead to the following, the 100th anniversary of American independence. Ask yourself which of these was inspired by freedom, that of Karl Marx whose economic system was patterned on the need for equality between the haves and the have-nots administered by tyrants or that of Auguste Bartholdi who cast in copper a mighty woman with a torch symbolizing an incentivized freedom and commemorated by Emma Lazarus as the mother of exiles.

Somewhere between the two America is witnessing its worst crisis of internal making she would ever face. Not far from Lady Liberty's honored flame her image will be dishonored in dung and urine by those who favor the authoritarian model.

Our final hope and last line of defense lies with the Tea Party patriot army of God to purge the system and reinstate a Judea-Christian morality or all is lost,

As night gives praise for the day
And freedom gives praise to God
Take this shield of one for its rejuvenative power
To refurbish the land for the return of
God's face and guiding hand.